FORT LAUDERDALE RECIPES

Collected and Published

By

The Fort Lauderdale Historical Society, Inc.

Fort Lauderdale, Florida

122487

Fort Lauderdale Historical Society
219 Southwest 2nd Avenue
Fort Lauderdale, Florida 33301

Printed in the United States of America
Rose Printing Company
Tallahassee, Florida

Fourth Printing in March, 1986

ACKNOWLEDGEMENTS

We extend many thanks to the ladies and gentlemen of the area for donating their favorite recipes for use in this book. Some of the recipes are originals, others are pioneer recipes, and some are just family favorites. The donor's name appears with his or her recipe.

Some recipes are listed as donated by "Recipe Selection Committee." In some cases several recipes for the same dish were received. The Committee arbitrarily picked the one to be used. When no acceptable recipes, or none at all, were received for certain dishes, we once again relied upon the experience of the members of that Committee to furnish a good recipe.

We wish to thank the following hard workers for the hours of labor and advice necessary to bring this book to you:

Mitchel J. Alles; Mrs. Alfred J. Beck; Dr. Frederick T. Boyd; Mrs. John A. Bossian, Jr.; Mrs. Arch Campbell; Mrs. Thomas Taylor Coon; Mrs. William G. Crawford;; Mrs. Ralph R. Lehr; Mrs. Robert S. Pendleton; Kenneth W. Ricklefs; Mrs. Dudley R. Stokes; Miss Louise Taylor and the staff of the Broward County Home Demonstration Agent Office; and Philip Weidling.

Our appreciation is also extended to Mrs. Ann M. Perry, author of **Dooryard Supermarket in the Tropics and Subtropics,** for permission to use some of her recipes, and to the Pachria Garden Club.

THE EDITOR

FORT LAUDERDALE RECIPES
COMMITTEE

Editor .... Mrs. Tom G. Lively

Recipe Selection Committee
    Chairman .... Mrs. Alfred J. Beck
    Co-Chairman .... Mrs. Robert S. Pendleton

Public Relations and Distribution
    Chairman .... Mrs. William G. Crawford

Proof Reading
    Chairman .... Mrs. Ralph R. Lehr

Advisor .... Mrs. Arch Campbell

CONTENTS

FORT LAUDERDALE — BRIEFLY

One of the many attractions of the Fort Lauderdale area is the year round harvest of fruits and vegetables, the fishing and hunting. This attraction is not just one of recent years but has lured the adventurer from the days when Spain held the peninsula. The reports and chronicles of early times speak of the Florida abundance.

Under Spanish rule from 1512 to 1762, Florida was the stopping place for hunters and fishermen from the other Spanish possessions. The Spanish used this area as a source of slave labor for the plantations of Cuba, so depleting the early Indians that today these Indian races are extinct. Yet, at times during the two centuries of Spanish rule, there were approximately 70 Franciscan priests and brothers with 44 missions and some 30,000 Indian converts. These Spaniards also named many of the places in Florida. During this period, the Spanish introduced nearly 200 cultivated plants.

From 1763 to 1783, Florida was under English rule. At the time of the take-over, there were about 6,500 Europeans living in Florida. Many left the country when the English rule began. England was anxious to repopulate with industrious English settlers and offered bounties on crops, grants of land and even subsidies. Two great reports were written on Florida at this time.

The first report was by John Gerard William DeBrahm, appointed in 1764 as Surveyor General of the Southern District of North America for George III of England. His work was entitled **History Of The Three Provinces, South Carolina, Georgia And East Florida.** It was in two volumns and accompanied by a map 25 feet long. DeBrahms renamed many of the areas, rivers, streams, bays of Florida. In some cases, the Spanish names were kept and some were anglo-saxonized.

The second report was that of Bernard Romans who was the Principal Deputy Surveyor for the Southern District of North America. It was called **A Concise Natural History Of East And West Florida.** Dated 1775, it records in great detail the vegetation, fish species and animal species found on his trips. He listed additional crops which might be of great value both at home and for export.

Florida took no part in the American Revolution of 1776, but was a place of refuge for thousands of Loyalists from the battling states.

When Great Britian and Spain went to war in 1779, the Spanish Governor of Louisiana invaded Florida and captured Pensacola. At the close of this war, Florida was once again given back to Spain. Spain held Florida only from 1783 to 1821.

In 1821, Florida became a United States Territory. During the years 1821 to 1835, there were many incidents with both runaway slaves and vengeful owners, Indians and settlers. These events brought on the period of the Second Seminole War, 1835 through 1842.

By the 1830's there were several families farming around New River. On the quiet Monday afternoon of January 6, 1836, the serenity of the farm community around the plantation of William Cooley was broken by the screams of children, the war cries of Indians and the sounds of rifle fire. On the north bank of New River, near today's Southwest 7th Avenue, the family of William Cooley consisting of his wife, three children and their tutor, were killed by a party of Seminoles. The house, coontie mill, sheds and cultivated orchards were burned. William Cooley, away at the time, was spared. Following the massacre, the New River settlement was abandoned.

In a petition to the United States Government for reimbursement of his losses, William Cooley listed his property and the following items of food: "2 barrels flour, 1 barrel pork, 1 barrel beef, 1 bag of coffee, 4 bags of corn, 1 barrel of grits, 1 barrel rice, 1 barrel salt, 21 gallons m. wine, a lot of sugar, a lot of butter, 16 barrels arrowroot, 10 boxes of arrowroot." Also listed as destroyed were, "6 acres planted in sugar cane, 2 acres Bermuda Arrowroot and the remaining 12 acres in corn, potatoes, pumpkin, etc." He also lost "80 head hogs, a lot of fowl and 5 sheeps, etc." The deposition of R. Fitzpatrick on William Cooley's losses also states his plantation had "a number of Valuable Fruit Trees of different kinds."

In February 1838, General Thomas S. Jesup, stationed at Fort Jupiter, ordered Major William Lauderdale and his Battalion of Tennessee Mounted Volunteers, along with a company of U.S. Artillery, to the site of New River to establish a fort. The fort was built and on March 16, 1838, General Jesup named it Fort Lauderdale after Major Lauderdale. This fort was abandoned that May but a subsequent fort was established on the beach and was active until 1842.

A list of provisions at the fort provides a clue to the eating habits of the men. An April 30th, 1841 Rations List shows the following: "15 barrels of pork, 2 barrels of beef, 292 pounds ham, 14 barrels flour, 2707 pounds hard bread, 12 bushels beans, 140 gallons whiskey, 179 pounds candles, 300 pounds soap, 5 bushels salt, 98 gallons vinegar, 450 pounds coffee, 1073 pounds sugar, 6 barrels sour kraut, 13 kegs pickled onions, 60 bushel potatoes, 10 bushels onions. The men supplimented these rations with fresh vegetables grown from seed issued by the Army. They also hunted and fished.

Lieutenant George H. Thomas arrived at Fort Lauderdale late in 1840. According to Freeman Cleaves in his book **Rock Of Chickamauga,** Thomas discovered the soldiers fishing for

> " . . . pompano, redfish, snappers and green turtles. The task of feeding the detachment fell on Thomas, who discovered he could stretch green-turtle steaks just so far. So much fine sea food was provided that the soldiers began to clamor for beef, which was scarce and poor in quality, and they even welcomed an occasional serving of barreled mess pork. Thomas devoted much of his time to the quest for supplies, entering the woods for deer and wild turkey."

In November 1841 Thomas went on two expeditions into the Everglades after Indians. Upon his return to the Fort, Thomas found a new commanding officer, Caption Erasmus Darwin Keyes whose first breakfast at Fort Lauderdale was:

> "muddy coffee without milk, brown sugar, hard bread, tough wheat cakes and semifluid rancid butter floating in a cracked teacup. For dinner bean soup was substituted for the buckwheat cakes and harsh commissary whiskey for the coffee. Thomas heard his complaints sympathetically and promptly set about getting together a decent bill of fare."

In 1845 Florida was declared a state. She remained part of the United States until 1861 when she joined the Confederate Union. At the end of the civil war, the State Legislature revoked the 1861 clause of session. Once again Florida became part of the United States.

In 1876 a line of Life-saving Stations was being built on the lower east coast. A "Notice of Completion" dated September 4, 1876 was filed for House of Refuge #4 which was here on the beach. This also was our first post office, a stop in the trip of the "Barefoot Mailman". Washington Jenkins was the first keeper of the station and arrived here with his family October 6, 1876. The nearest white neighbors were the station keepers at Station #5, 20 miles to the south or at Station #3 which was 24 miles north.

Increasing numbers of people were coming to Florida. Glowing reports were sent of the fabulous catches, mouth-watering food and Shangri-La living. In 1878 Dr. James A. Henshall made a trip down the eastern coast of Florida traveling from Titusville to the Keys. Enchanted with the area he made a second trip in 1881. One of the many comments he made on our area:

> "New River for six miles above its mouth is the straightest, deepest and finest river I have seen in Florida although a narrow one. It is famous for its shark (regular man-eaters, some of them), and for the immense number and variety of its fishes.
>
> Rushing in and out with the tide, at New River, fishes can be seen by the thousands, which snap at anything, even a bit of rag tied to the hook and thrown to them by a strong hand-line.
>
> Six miles above the inlet is the "Haulover" opposite the site of old Fort Lauderdale, and marked by a group of coconut trees."

By late 1892 the sand road from Palm Beach to Miami had been completed. In January 1893, Frank Stranahan arrived here to operate the ferry across New River and to run an over-night camp. The trip from Palm Beach to Miami took two days and at New River accommodations were made for the stop-over. The ferry and camp were located at the site of the present day Pioneer House. Stranahan later extended his operations to include a post office and trading post. In 1895 Flagler extended the East Coast Railroad from West Palm Beach to Miami. The opening in 1896 brought many more settlers to Fort Lauderdale.

The first census of people living in the Fort Lauderdale community was in 1900 and reveals 52 residents. The growth is recorded in the following census figures:

1910	143	1945	26,185
1915	1,870	1950	36,328
1920	2,065	1955	62,906
1925	5,625	1960	81,806
1930	8,666	1970	139,590
1935	9,222	1980	153,279
1940	17,996		

In 1911 the people of the area formed the incorporated Town of Fort Lauderdale. By 1917 there were enough residents to form a city. The City of Fort Lauderdale was incorporated June 4, 1917.

As of 1986, Fort Lauderdale has a population of approximately 156,000 and is still growing. We hope you will enjoy growing with us and that this book will help you relish the bountiful foods found here.

—Lucille Lively

TROPICAL FRUIT AND NUT LIST

This list was compiled only to serve as a guide. We tried to pick the most popular backyard fruits and nuts as well as the most hardy growers. Please remember that many of our tropical fruits are extremely rich foods. Some can not be eaten until fully ripe. They do spoil quickly so never use "over ripe" fruits. All of our fruits should be **tree-picked**. The fruits which have dropped on the ground should not be used.

Avocado or Alligator Pear (Persea americana) - eaten right from tree, peeled and seed removed, sliced for salads; used also in soups, dips, spreads, frozen desserts.

Akee (Blighia sapida) - must be fully ripe when picked. When split, white fleshy part is edible; also boiled, fried.

Banana (Musa paradisica) - eaten right from tree, peeled; also used in salads, baked, fried, broiled, in desserts; dried and flour made; unripe fruit used in cooking. Many uses.

*Barbados Cherry (Malpighia glabra) - eaten picked from bush as you would a cherry, discarding inside seed; used in jams, jellies, sauces.

*Bignay (Antidesma bunius) - tangy fruit used mostly in punches, jellies.

Calamondin Orange (Citrus mitis) - used like regular orange or lime in punches, used as decoration, preserved also.

Canistel or Egg Fruit (Lecuma nervosa) - eaten from tree with little lime juice and butter. Sliced in half, seed discarded and flesh scooped out; also used in sauces, fried.

*Capulin or Jam-fruit (Muntingia calabura) - eaten from tree also used in jams, tarts, desserts.

Carambola (Averrhoa carambola) - eaten right from tree, sliced as decoration in salads, punches, preserved.

*Carissa or Natal Plum (Carissa grandiflora) - may be eaten right from tree, usually cut in half, seeds removed, used in salads, jellies.

Ceylon Peach (Prunus persica) - used as regular peach, eaten from tree or used in salads, desserts, jams, sauces.

*Ceylon Gooseberry (Dovyalis hebecarpa) - used in punches, jams, and jellies.

Chayote (sechium edule) - used like squash, peeled, sliced or diced and then cooked, fried or baked.

Coconut (Cocos nucifera) - outer husk, inner husk must be removed. Used in many ways, eaten fresh from tree, unripe coconut also eaten, used in salads, desserts, punches, dried, baked, etc.

*Cocoplum (Chrysobalanus icaco) - native to Florida. Usually peeled and cooked, used in sauces, preserves. Seed inside can be roasted and eaten as nuts.

Custard Apple (Annona reticulata) - native to Florida. Eaten fresh from tree, cut in half, stem, core and remove seeds. The pulp may be eaten with spoon or cut up and served as dessert. Also used in punches, sauces, puddings.

Grapefruit (Citrus paradisi) - eaten fresh from tree, peeled and segments eaten or sliced in half and flesh eaten with spoon. Used in many ways, in salads, desserts, punches.

*Guava (Psidium guajva) - Ruby Guava may be eaten along with several others but best cooked, stewed, preserved, in sauces and punches.

*Governor's Plum or Ramontchi (Flacourtia indica) - must be picked ripe to be best eating. Can also be used in jelly.

*Grumichama (Eugenia dombeyi) - eaten like cherries from the tree, discarding the seeds. Used in place of cherries.

*Hill Gooseberry or Downey Myrtle (Rhodomyrtus tomentosa) - eaten from bush as you would a gooseberry. Used in place of gooseberries.

Horseradish Tree or Moringa (Moringa oleifers) - pods, leaves and flowers, young roots are all used. Pods, leaves and flowers used as curry vegetable. Young roots are used as horseradish substitute.

*Indian Jujube (Zizyphus mauritiana) - eaten from tree discarding seed. Can be stewed, used in sauces, jellies and dried.

*Jaboticaba (Myciaria cauliflora) - eaten from tree discarding tough skin. Also used in jellies and jams.

*Jack Fruit (Artocarpus integra) - cut in half and pulp is eaten fresh. Also preserved and dried. Seeds may be roasted and eaten like nuts.

*Jambolan Plum (Syzygium cumini) - sometimes eaten but mostly used in jams and jellies.

*Jelly Palm (Butia capitata) - eaten off the tree like a miniature apple.

Kumquat (Fortunella spp.) - eaten right from the tree, used as decorations, used in sauces, preserves, pickled and candied.

*Key Lime (Citrus aurantifolia) - more acid than the lemon or Persian Lime used as flavoring, in punches, in cooking, in sauces and instead of vinegar.

Lemon (Citrus limon) - used in flavoring, in punches, in cooking, in sauces, instead of vinegar.

*Loquat (Eriobotrya japonica) - eaten fresh from tree, also used in desserts, jellies, sauces.

*Lychee (Litchi chinensis) - eaten fresh from tree, also dried.

Macadamia or Queensland Nut (Macadamia ternifolia) - eaten from tree and also roasted. The outside covering and hard inside shell must be cracked and the edible nut is the inside white kernel.

*Mamey or Mammee Apple (Mammea americana) - eaten from tree, peeled and flesh cut away from seed. Also stewed, used in desserts, sauces, preserves.

*Mango (Mangifera indica) - eaten from tree, peeled and flesh cut away from seed. Used in salads, punches, desserts, relishes, preserves, in chutneys. Used unripe in many recipes.

Orange (Citrus spp.) - eaten from tree, peeled and segments eaten or sliced used in many ways, as flavoring in cooking, punches, desserts, in sauces, candied, etc.

Papaya (Carica papaya) - eaten from tree, peeled and flesh sliced. Seeds are also eaten. Used in salads, punches, desserts, meat tenderizer, preserved, cooked, etc.

Pigeon pea (Cajanus indicus-Fabaceae) - Pods are opened and peas inside are used in cooking, in soups, as main dish.

*****Pigeon Plum (Cocolobis floridana)** - native to Florida. Can be eaten from the tree but is usually used in jellies and jams, sauces.

Pineapple (Ananas comosus) - eaten fresh from bush, peeled and sliced, tough inner core discarded. Used as flavoring in cooking, in punches, desserts, jams, preserves, candied, etc.

Pitomba (Eugenia luschnathiana) - eaten fresh from tree. Used in jams, jellies, desserts, sauces.

Pomegranate (Punica granatum) - sometimes eaten from tree, peeled, juice sacs eaten and seeds discarded. Usually used in punches, sauces, jams.

*****Rose Apple (Syzygium jambos)** - eaten fresh from tree discarding seeds and core. Used in salads, preserved, cooked, in jams, jellies, candied - smells and tastes like a rose.

*****Roselle or Jamaica Sorrel or Florida Cranberry (Hibiscus sabadarif-fa)** - used as you would cranberry for sauces, jellies, preserves, in punches, desserts, dried. Seeds may be roasted and eaten like nuts. Leaves may be used in salads.

*****Sapodilla (Achras sapota)** - eaten fresh from tree, peeled and seeds discarded. Must be fully ripe when picked. Used also as syrups, in desserts, vinegars. Flavor is similar to that of a pear.

*****Sea Grape (Cocolobis uvifera)** - native to Florida. Sometimes eaten fresh from bush as you would a grape but usually used in jellies, syrups, punches.

Star Apple (Chrysophyllum cainito) - eaten fresh from tree, rind removed and pulp eaten discarding seeds. Slight chilling improves flavor. Pulp used as a dessert.

Strawberry Tree (Myrica ruba) - usually eaten fresh from tree. Used as you would a strawberry, as a fruit, dessert, etc.

Sugar Apple or Sweetsop (Annona squamosa) - must be picked exactly ripe. Eaten fresh from tree, broken into segments and scooped from rind. Used as a dessert. May be used in cooking.

*****Surinan Cherry (Eugenia uniflora)** - eaten from bush as you would a cherry. Used in desserts, punches, in jams, jellies, etc.

*****Tamarind (Tamarindus indica)** - eaten fresh from tree, peeling pod. Used in sauces, preserves, curries, chutney, cooked and eaten as vegetable. Used unripe in cooking. Many uses.

* These are hardy growers for the Broward County area.

THE PIONEER HOUSE, FORT LAUDERDALE, FLORIDA

Beverages

Polly, put the kettle on,
Polly, put the kettle on,
Polly, put the kettle on,
We'll all have tea.

— Polly, Put the Kettle On
Nursery Rhyme
Anonymous

THICK BANANA NOG (4 - 12 ounce glasses)

(Mrs. Tom G. Lively)

3 ripe bananas
2 cups pineapple juice

1 package frozen sliced
strawberries

1. Mash bananas in large bowl. Partially defrost strawberries. Mash into banana mixture. Add pineapple juice. Mix well.
2. Pour over ice cubes.

NOTE: If have blender, put bananas, strawberries into blender at low speed for about 1 minute. Add pineapple juice. Blend for 30 seconds. Pour over ice cubes.

STRAWBERRY SHRUB

(Recipe Selection Committee)

12 pounds fruit
2 quarts water

5 ounces tartaric acid
Powdered sugar

1. Put acid into water and mix. Place fruit in jar. Pour acid water over fruit. Let stand for 48 hours. Strain (but do not bruise fruit).
2. Measure juice. Add 1½ pounds powdered sugar for each pint of fruit juice. Let stand for 48 hours, stirring once a day.
3. Pour juice into bottle and cork lightly. (If ferments, leave cork out few days.) Keep bottles standing upright.

GUAVA JUICE AND JELLY BASE

(Recipe Selection Committee)

2 quarts firm ripe guavas
2 quarts water

2 quarts green guavas

1. Wash guavas. Remove blossom end and stem end and any blemishes. Slice.
2. Add guavas to water and boil. Reduce heat and cook for about 20 minutes.
3. Strain through jelly bag.
4. Reheat juice and pour into hot sterile jars, seal.

NOTE: For beverage dilute with equal amount of water. Add sugar or other fruit to taste. This is also base for jelly.

PAPAYA SHAKE

(U. of Fla. Agr. Ext. Service
Circular 162)

2 cups mashed ripe papaya
¼ cup lime juice
1 teaspoon nutmeg

⅔ cup sugar
1½ cups evaporated milk
1½ cups water

1. Combine mashed fruit and sugar. Add lime juice, nutmeg, water and milk. Chill.
2. To serve, shake with cracked ice and pour into glasses.

FRESH LIMEADE

(U. of Fla. Ext. Service
Circular 167)

6 limes
1 lime sliced thin

¾ cup sugar
4 cups water

1. Wash limes. Cut in half and squeeze juice. Pour into large container. Add sugar and water. Stir. Chill.
2. To serve, pour over ice cubes. Put 1 lime slice in each glass.

NOTE: This can be used for lemon, calamondin, or sour orange ades.

BLACKBERRY ACID

(Recipe Selection Committee)

1 gallon blackberries
Sugar

1 ounce tartaric acid

1. Put berries in stone crock. Cover with water. Add acid. Let stand for 24 hours.
2. Strain and measure the resultant juice.
3. For each pint of juice, add one pound of sugar. Put in pan and boil for 20 minutes. Pour into hot sterile bottles and seal.
4. To serve, chill, dilute with water or pour over crushed ice.

TAMARIND-ADE

(Broward County Home
Demonstration Agent)

1 cup tamarind syrup
6 sprigs mint

4¾ cups water

1. Mix syrup and water. Chill.
2. Fill glasses ¼ with cracked ice. Fill with chilled tamarind mix. Put sprig of mint in each glass.

SYLLABUB

(Recipe Selection Committee)

1 pint heavy cream
½ cup sugar

½ cup light cream
½ cup wine (or brandy)

1. Mix heavy cream and light cream. Add sugar and wine.
2. Churn in Syllabub churn or beat with egg whip until foamy.
3. Serve immediately.

EGG NOG

(Recipe Selection Committee)

4 eggs
4 cups milk
Dash nutmeg

3 tablespoons sugar
1 teaspoon vanilla

1. Separate eggs. Beat yolks with sugar. Add milk and vanilla, mix well.
2. Beat whites until stiff. Fold into yolk mixture.
3. Ladle into cups and top with dash nutmeg.

COFFEE COOLER

(Recipe Selection Committee)

2 cups strong black coffee

1 pint ice cream (vanilla)

1. Put ice cream into bowl. Beat coffee into ice cream. Spoon into tall glasses (4 tall glasses or 6 short glasses) and serve at once.

MOCHA DRINK

(Recipe Selection Committee)

1 square unsweetened
    chocolate (1 ounce)
1½ cups milk

1½ cups hot strong coffee
3 tablespoons sugar
¼ cup whipping cream

1. Chop chocolate. Add sugar and ½ cup milk. Heat until chocolate is melted. Add remaining milk and bring to boil. Simmer about 5 minutes. Add coffee.
2. Whip cream. Pour chocolate-coffee mixture into cups and top with whipped cream.

CRANBERRY TEA (about 24 cups)

(Mrs. R. C. McGuire)

Base:

1 pound cranberries
1 quart water
3 cups sugar

1 pint hot water
3 tablespoons "Red Hots" sauce

1. Boil cranberries until soft and then put through sieve.
2. Mix sugar, water and hot sauce until dissolved.
3. Mix cranberry pulp with sugar water, bring to boil.

Tea:

1 pint cranberry base
Juice 4 oranges

3 quarts water
Juice 2 lemons

1. Mix cranberry base, orange juice, lemon juice and water.
2. Strain mixture into kettle.
3. Heat mixture and serve hot.

TOMATO JUICE COCKTAIL

(Recipe Selection Committee)

1 peck ripe tomatoes
4 tablespoons salt
⅛ teaspoon nutmeg
½ teaspoon "Red Hots" sauce or
chili powder

1 cup sugar
⅛ teaspoon cinnamon
4 tablespoons vinegar

1. Put tomatoes in kettle. Cover with water and bring to boil. Strain. You should have one gallon of juice.
2. Put back into pot. Add salt, nutmeg, sugar, cinnamon, hot sauce, vinegar and bring to boil. Pour into sterile jars and seal.
3. To serve, chill (may be served immediately after cooking — just chill instead of bottling).

SPICED COCOA

(Recipe Selection Committee)

¼ cup cocoa
⅛ teaspoon cinnamon
2 cups water
½ teaspoon vanilla

¼ cup sugar
⅛ teaspoon ground cloves
1 can evaporated milk
(13½ ounce)

1. Mix cocoa, sugar, cinnamon, cloves. Add water. Bring to boil. Boil 5 minutes.
2. Add milk to cocoa mix and bring **to** boil. **Do not** boil.
3. Serve at once. Can be topped with whipped cream or one large marshmallow.

SPICED TEA

(Mrs. Wm. G. Crawford)

3 quarts freshly boiled water
1½ cups sugar
½ cup lemon juice

2 tablespoons orange pekoe tea
1½ cups orange juice
1 cup spiced water

1. Pour boiling water over tea and steep 5 minutes. Strain. Add sugar and stir until dissolved. Add strained fruit juices, add spiced water.
2. Either re-heat to serve hot or chill to serve cold.

Spiced Water:

1 cup water
1 teaspoon allspice

1 teaspoon whole cloves
1 stick cinnamon (1 inch long)

1. Add allspice, cloves and cinnamon to water. Bring to boil. Reduce heat and simmer 5 minutes. Strain.

NOTE: Spiced water may be made a day ahead and stored in glass jar in refrigerator.

MOTHER'S RUSSIAN TEA

(Mrs. Robert K. Lowry and Mrs. Keith Sullivan)

16 tablespoons tea
3 quarts water
2 cups sugar
2 sticks cinnamon

2 tablespoons whole cloves
Grated rind and juice of 3 oranges and 2 lemons

1. Boil water. Add tea and let steep 5 minutes. Strain or remove tea bags.
2. Put cinnamon and cloves in spice bag. Add sugar and spice bag to tea. Let stand 10 minutes or until spicy enough. Remove spice bag.
3. Just before serving add fruit juice and rind. (Taste and if not sweet enough, add more sugar.)

SWITZEL TEA

(Recipe Selection Committee)

1 gallon cold water
2 cups sugar

1 cup cider vinegar
1 tablespoon grated nutmeg

1. Mix all ingredients. Serve cold.

FRUIT PUNCH (serves 50 - 60)

(Mrs. Wm. G. Crawford)

1 quart pineapple juice
1 quart orange juice

1 quart apple juice
2 quarts ginger ale

1. Mix the juices and let stand for at least 2 hours.
2. When ready to serve, pour in ginger ale. Serve over block of ice.

CRANBERRY PUNCH

(Mrs. Dwight L. Rogers, Jr.)

6 cups cranberry juice
1½ cups orange juice
2 bottles ginger ale (1 pint 12 ounce size)

3 cups apple juice
¾ cup lemon juice

1. Mix all fruit juices. Chill.
2. When ready to serve, add ginger ale. Pour over ice mold in large punch bowl.
3. Mold of ice may be made by freezing red maraschino cherries in water.

NOTE: For Christmas, use red and green cherries in ice mold.

FRENCH PUNCH (about 2 gallons)

(Mrs. W. T. Crawford)

2 cups lime juice
1 stick cinnamon
1 quart pineapple juice
2 quarts water

2 cups sugar
6 whole cloves
2 packages frozen strawberries

1. In pan cook lime juice and sugar. Boil 5 minutes. Put cinnamon and cloves in bag. Drop into lime juice and boil 5 more minutes. Remove spice bag.
2. Put lime syrup into pineapple juice. Add water and strawberries. Chill and serve.

THE BEACH AT FORT LAUDERDALE, FLORIDA

Breads

Give us day by day our daily bread.

Holy Bible
Luke 11:3

SPOON BREAD

(Mrs. Gilbert B. Dickey, Jr.)

4 cups milk
2 tablespoons butter
4 eggs, well beaten

1 cup fine corn meal
1⅓ teaspoons salt

1. Scald milk in double boiler.
2. Gradually stir in corn meal and cook until the consistency of mush.
3. Add butter and salt.
4. In bowl beat eggs.
5. Slowly pour corn meal mixture over eggs, mixing constantly.
6. Pour into well greased 1½ quart baking dish.
7. Bake at 425° for 45 minutes.

NOTE: This has a wonderful custard-like consistency.

STICK-TO-THE-RIBS BREAD

(Mrs. Tom G. Lively)

1 package yeast
2 tablespoons honey
⅔ cup dry milk
2 tablespoons corn oil
½ cup soy flour

1½ cups warm water
1 teaspoon salt
1 egg
½ cup wheat germ
4 cups unbleached flour

1. Dissolve yeast in water and let stand 5 minutes.
2. In bowl mix egg, honey, oil, salt, dry milk. Add **wheat germ**, yeast and soy flour. Mix well. Add white flour.
3. On floured board, knead until shiny. Form into ball and put into greased bowl. Cover, let rise in warm place 1 hour. Punch down, knead and form into ball and let rise again for about 1 hour.
4. Punch down, divide into two balls. Form each into loaf shape and put into greased bread tins.
5. Put tins in cold oven and let stand for about 30 minutes.
6. Turn oven on to 375° and bake for about 50 minutes. Cool slightly before removing from pans.

NOTE: If your oven takes a long time to warm up do **not leave tins in** oven while heating. This is solid bread, not airy. Slice thin.

DILLY CASSEROLE BREAD

(Mrs. Rowena Bullock)

1 package dry yeast
1 cup creamed cottage cheese (heated lukewarm)
1 tablespoon butter
1 teaspoon salt
1 egg
¼ cup warm water

2 tablespoons sugar
1 tablespoon instant minced onion
2 teaspoons dill seed
¼ teaspoon soda
2½ cups all purpose flour

1. Soften yeast in water. In bowl combine warm cottage cheese, egg, sugar, onion, butter, dill seed, salt, soda and yeast.
2. Add flour to form stiff dough. Cover dish and let rise in warm place until light and double in volume (1-2 hours).
3. Punch down dough. Turn into well greased 8 inch round casserole dish. Let rise in warm place until double in volume (40-60 minutes).
4. Bake at 350° for 40-50 minutes or until golden brown. Remove from oven and brush top with melted butter.

NOTE: No kneading is necessary. This is even better toasted — if there is any left!

GINGER BREAD

(Mrs. Alfred J. Beck)

½ cup sugar
2½ cups flour
⅛ teaspoon ground cloves
½ teaspoon salt
2 teaspoons baking powder
2 eggs

½ cup butter
1 teaspoon ginger, ground
1 teaspoon cinnamon
2 teaspoons soda
1 cup buttermilk
1 cup ALAGA syrup

1. Mix sugar, flour, ginger, cloves, cinnamon, salt, baking powder.
2. Add soda to buttermilk and add to flour mixture, add syrup and butter. Beat eggs well and add.
3. Pour into greased oblong baking pan and bake for 30 minutes at 350°.

BANANA BREAD

(Mrs. R. H. Gore, Sr.
by Mrs. Joseph A. Gore)

3 large bananas
2 eggs
½ cup sugar
½ cup butter

½ cup buttermilk
1 teaspoon soda
2 cups pastry flour
Dash salt

1. Mash bananas (potato masher or blender). **Add eggs,** sugar, butter and buttermilk.
2. Sift soda and flour. Add gradually to egg mixture and mix thoroughly. Put dash salt into mix.
3. Pour into well greased pan (not bread tin). **Size 6x10x2** inch is good size.
4. Bake for 50 to 60 minutes at 350°.
5. Cool on rack and for easier slicing put into **refrigerator** for about 4 hours.

NOTE: This freezes well and also is wonderful toasted.

~~~~~~~~~~~~~~~~~~

EGGBREAD (serves 4)

(Mrs. Gilbert B. Dickey, Jr.)

2 eggs
2 heaping teaspoons baking powder
4 tablespoons flour

½ teaspoon salt
¾ cup milk
1 cup cornmeal
1½ tablespoons cooking oil

1. Break eggs in bowl. Beat well. **Add salt and baking** powder. Stir well.
2. Add milk and sift in the flour while stirring. **Add corn-** meal and oil, stirring well.
3. Grease 8x8 inch square pan and put in 450° oven until pan is hot.
4. Pour batter into hot greased pan.
5. Bake for approx. 25 minutes at 450°, or until done.

NOTE: Wonderful with butter or as base for toppings. **See Chicken and** Eggbread also.

CHEESE BISCUITS

(Mrs. John H. Kremer)

½ pound grated medium-sharp cheese

½ pound butter (2 sticks)

⅛ teaspoon red pepper

½ pound plain flour

½ teaspoon salt

1. Melt butter in mixing bowl over hot water.
2. Sift flour, salt, pepper and add grated cheese. Mix melted butter thoroughly in flour mix.
3. Chill overnight in refrigerator.
4. When needed slice off piece of dough. Handle just enough to blend and roll out on floured board. Cut with small biscuit cutter.
5. Place on ungreased cookie sheet. Pierce each biscuit with fork.
6. Bake about 12 minutes at 350°. Do not let get too brown.
7. Drain on paper toweling. When cold sprinkle with sugar.
8. May be stored by packing in air-tight jars putting waxed paper between each layer of biscuit.

GARLIC BREAD

(Recipe Selection Committee)

½ stick butter

1 loaf French bread, or Italian bread

1 clove garlic crushed

Dash paprika

Dash parsley

1. Let butter stand at room temperature until soft. Mix in crushed garlic clove.
2. Slice bread but do not cut all the way through. Spread garlic butter between each slice.
3. Brush top with garlic butter, dash paprika and sprinkle parsley bits over top.
4. Wrap in foil paper.
5. Put in oven for 15 minutes at 350° or until bread is warm and butter soaked in.

BACON RING BISCUITS

(Mrs. James F. Smalley)

2 cups flour
2 teaspoons baking powder
¾ cup milk
10-12 slices cooked bacon
   finely chopped

½ teaspoon salt
⅓ cup shortening
⅓ pound butter

1. Sift flour, measure. Add baking powder, salt. Cut in shortening with fork until flour is crumbly. Add milk until mixture is moist but not too sticky.
2. On well floured board, roll dough very thin.
3. Mix butter and bacon. Spread on dough. Roll dough as for jelly roll. Chill in refrigerator for about 2-3 hours.
4. Slice ¼ to ½ inch thick. Place on ungreased baking sheet.
5. Bake for 10-15 minutes at 450°.

STIR-N-ROLL BISCUITS (12 biscuits)

(Mrs. Ralph R. Lehr)

2 cups sifted all purpose flour
1 teaspoon salt
⅔ cup milk

3 teaspoons baking powder
⅓ cup salad oil

1. Sift together flour, baking powder and salt. Add oil to milk. Pour into flour. Stir with fork until mixture cleans side of bowl.
2. Smooth the dough by kneading about 10 times. Do not add more flour.
3. Put dough on waxed paper. Press out to ¼ inch thick with hands. (For higher biscuit roll out ½ inch thick.)
4. Cut out with unfloured cookie cutter. Place on ungreased cookie sheet.
5. Bake 10 to 12 minutes at 475°.

RIZ BISCUITS

(Mrs. Harry H. Smith)

2½ cups self-rising flour   4 tablespoons shortening
1 cup buttermilk   1 package yeast dissolved in
1 tablespoon sugar   some warm water

1. Sift flour. Add sugar. Work in shortening. Add milk and yeast.
2. Quickly cut into biscuits and let rise in warm place until double in bulk (about 30 to 60 minutes).
3. Bake on cookie sheet at 375° until brown, or about 15 to 20 minutes.

ALABAMA BISCUITS

(Mrs. Wm. E. Brooks)

4 cups flour   ½ cup shortening
¼ cup warm water   2 teaspoons baking powder
2 teaspoons sugar   1 cake yeast (or 1 package)
1 teaspoon salt   ½ stick butter
1 cup milk

1. Sift flour and measure. Add sugar, salt, baking powder. Mix well. Mix shortening into flour.
2. Dissolve yeast in warm water. Add milk. Add to flour mix.
3. Turn onto well floured board and roll to ½ inch thick. Cut into biscuits.
4. Melt butter. Grease bottom and sides of pan. Then dip biscuits into butter. Place in rows on pan. Let rise in warm place until double in size (at least 1 hour).
5. Bake for 15 minutes at 350° or until done.

POTATO-YEAST ROLLS (6 dozen)

(Mrs. Alfred J. Beck)

To Make Yeast:

1 cup mashed potatoes
1 cup warm potato water
1 cup cold water

1 cup sugar
1 package yeast

1. Dissolve yeast in warm potato water. Add potatoes, sugar and cold water. Mix. Let stand 3 hours before using.

To Make Rolls:

3 eggs
3 cups yeast mix
1 cup salad oil

9 cups flour (or 4½ cups white and 4¼ cups whole wheat)
1 teaspoon salt

1. Mix eggs, oil and yeast mix. Add flour and mix well.
2. Knead dough on floured board until it reaches a smooth (shiny) rolling consistency. Cut with small biscuit cutter.
3. Put on greased cookie sheet.
4. Bake 15-20 minutes at 375°. (Oven should be pre-heated.)

NOTE: Extra rolls keep well if put in plastic bag and put in refrigerator, they re-heat well, may be toasted on a spider, delicious base for creamed dishes. They are also excellent for "passing among your neighbors!"

POPOVERS (8)

(Recipe Selection Committee)

2 eggs
2 tablespoons oil
¼ teaspoon salt

1 cup milk
1 cup sifted flour

1. Heat oven. Turn to 450° (use oven thermometer to make sure temperature reaches 450° before starting to make Popovers). Grease muffin tins and put in oven.
2. Put eggs, oil, milk, salt in bowl. Beat until well mixed. Beat in flour. Use rotary beater and beat for two minutes (or put in blender and blend for 1 minute at high speed).
3. Pull hot tin out of oven. Fill half full with batter and put back in oven.
4. Bake for 10 minutes at 450°. Reduce heat to 350° and bake for 35 minutes longer.
5. To keep popovers hot, slit sides and keep in warming oven until ready to serve.

CINNAMON FRUIT ROLLS

(Mrs. Leigh F. Robinson)

1 cake yeast
½ cup milk, scalded
¼ cup sugar
1 egg, beaten
Butter
2 tablespoons cinnamon
¼ cup nuts

½ cup lukewarm water
¼ cup shortening
2 teaspoons salt
3¼ cups flour
½ cup brown sugar
¼ cup raisins
¼ cup chopped citron

1. Dissolve yeast in water. Pour scalded milk over shortening. Add ¼ cup sugar and the salt. Stir until well mixed. Add egg and yeast mixture. Add flour. Mix well.
2. Put dough in greased bowl, cover and let rise in warm place. When doubled in bulk (about 1 hour), punch down, brush with some melted butter, cover and put in refrigerator.
3. When ready to use dough remove from refrigerator and allow to warm slightly. Roll ¼ inch thick into rectangular shape.
4. Spread with melted butter and sugar, cinnamon, raisins, nuts and citron. Roll as for jelly roll. Cut with knife dipped in flour into 1 inch slices.
5. Place cut side up on greased baking sheet.
6. Allow to rise until double in bulk.
7. Bake for 15-20 minutes at 400°.

BRAN MUFFINS (12)

(Mrs. Tom G. Lively)

1¾ cups flour
¾ cup bran
3 teaspoons baking powder
¼ teaspoon salt

1 cup milk
1 egg
4 tablespoons oil
¼ cup molasses

1. Sift flour and measure. Sift with baking powder, salt then add bran.
2. Lightly beat egg. Add molasses, oil, milk. Gradually add flour to egg mixture.
3. Pour mixture into greased muffin tins. Fill only half full.
4. Bake 25 minutes at 400°

CRANBERRY MUFFINS (12 large)

(Mrs. Robert S. Pendleton)

¼ cup shortening
2 eggs
5 teaspoons baking powder
⅔ cup milk
¼ cup sugar

2 cups sifted all purpose flour
1 teaspoon salt
1 cup whole cranberry sauce
   (well drained)

1. Cream the shortening and sugar. Beat eggs, add.
2. Sift flour, baking powder, salt. Alternate flour and milk while stirring into egg mix.
3. In greased muffin tin, pour batter ⅓ full. Add 1 teaspoon cranberries to center of each muffin. Add ⅓ more batter (making each cup total of ⅔ full).
4. Bake for 30 minutes at 400°.

COFFEE CAKE

(Mrs. Arthur Ward,
Pachira Garden Club)

1½ cups flour
1 teaspoon salt
¾ cup sugar
½ cup milk
½ cup brown sugar
½ teaspoon cinnamon
½ cup chopped nut meats

3 teaspoons baking powder
1 teaspoon vanilla
¼ cup butter
1 egg
2 tablespoons flour
2 tablespoons melted butter

1. Cream sugar and butter. Add milk, egg and mix. Add vanilla.
2. Sift flour with baking powder, salt. Add gradually to the milk mixture.
3. Mix melted butter, cinnamon, brown sugar, flour and nuts.
4. Pour half the batter into greased 9 inch square pan. Put butter-nut mixture on top of batter. Pour remaining batter over the butter-nut mix.
5. Bake for 35 minutes at 375°.

APRICOT NUT COFFEE CAKE

(Recipe Selection Committee)

2 cups dried apricots
2 cups water
1 egg, beaten
1 cup sugar
2 tablespoons butter
¾ cup orange juice

2 cups sifted flour
3 teaspoons baking powder
¼ teaspoon soda
¼ teaspoon salt
1 cup chopped nut meats

1. Soak apricots in water for 1 hour. Remove and chop fine. Put apricot pieces back in water. Add beaten egg, orange juice. Melt butter and add.
2. Mix flour, baking powder, soda, salt. Blend flour into apricot mixture. Add nut meats.
3. Pour into flat baking dish, well greased.
4. Bake for 60 minutes at 350°.

KLYNER

(Mrs. Donald C. Little)

4 cups flour
3 tablespoons cream
2 tablespoons butter
1 teaspoon dry ammonia

3 eggs
1 cup sugar
1 teaspoon baking powder

1. Mix butter, cream, eggs. Add flour, sugar, baking powder and dry ammonia (If you can purchase this, if not, the Klyner will not be as crisp).
2. Roll out thin, about ¼ inch and cut into long strips 2½ inches wide. Then cut strips diagonally into 3 inch long pieces. Make a longwise slit in middle of strip and tuck one end through this.
3. Fry in hot deep fat until brown. Drain on paper towel.

YORKSHIRE PUDDING (serves 12)

(Mrs. C. W. Schlueter)

⅔ cup flour   1 egg

¾ cup milk   Beef fat

1. Beat egg, milk, flour together. Should be consistency of thick cream. Beat well. Put aside for about 1 hour.
2. Melt beef fat. Put 1 large teaspoon of fat into each muffin tin (tin size 2¼ inches in diameter).
3. Heat oven to 465°. Put muffin tin in oven. When fat is smoldering hot, take tin out of oven.
4. Add two tablespoons cold water to batter. Beat well. Pour batter into hot tin.
5. Put in oven for 20-25 minutes at 465°.

HUSH PUPPIES

(Mrs. Nelson B. Thomas)

1 cup cornmeal   ¼ cup milk (or water)

2 teaspoons baking powder   1 small chopped onion

½ teaspoon salt   (optional)

1 egg

1. Mix cornmeal, baking powder, salt and onion.
2. Break egg into mix and beat vigorously. Add milk and beat.
3. Form into small balls (about the size of a walnut).
4. Drop into deep hot fat (400°) and fry until brown. Serve hot.

PAN CAKES SUPREME (18 dollar-size cakes)

(Mrs. E. R. Davis,
Pachira Garden Club)

3 eggs, separated
¼ teaspoon salt
⅓ cup flour

8 ounces or 1 cup creamed
cottage cheese

1. Beat egg whites stiff.
2. Beat egg yolks until creamy and thick.
3. Stir salt, flour and cottage cheese into yolks.
4. Blend well. Fold in whipped egg whites.

SOURDOUGH HOT CAKES (serves 4)

(Mrs. Tom G. Lively)

1 pint sourdough starter
(see below)
1 tablespoon sugar

2 eggs
Baking soda

1. Heat griddle and grease.
2. In bowl mix starter, sugar and eggs. Batter should be slightly thick. Adjust by adding milk or flour.
3. **Tricky Part:** Sprinkle one teaspoonful of baking soda into batter and mix. (This is to neutralize sour batter and to make hotcakes rise.) Batter should foam.
4. Taste a bit of batter. If tastes real sour, add a little more baking soda.
5. Fry brown on griddle and serve at once.

Sourdough Starter: Two methods

1. Mix equal parts flour and water. Put in glass jar or crock. Keep in warm place about 10 days or until sours. (This is a little hard in Florida.)
2. Stir 2 cups flour, two tablespoons sugar, one tablespoon salt, one tablespoon vinegar together. Add enough water to make a thin batter. Put in crock and let stand in warm place for 10 days.

After starter has turned sour, the crock may be kept in refrigerator. When using, warm starter to room temperature. Always add more flour and water when you take some "starter" out. This keeps "starter" going.

NOTE: A good base for hotcakes, bread, rolls.

THE WOMAN'S CLUB, FORT LAUDERDALE, FLORIDA

Cakes and Cookies

Pat-a-cake, pat-a-cake, baker's man,
Bake me a cake as fast as you can . . . .

Pat-A-Cake
Nursery Rhyme
Anonymous

100 YEAR OLD POUND CAKE

(Mrs. Wm. H. Marshall)

1 pound sugar
9 large eggs (or 10 small eggs)
1 pound butter

1 pound flour
1 teaspoon lemon extract

1. Cream the sugar and butter. Separate the eggs. Beat egg yolks and add to butter mix. Add lemon extract. Mix well.
2. Add flour gradually.
3. Beat egg whites until stiff. Fold into flour mixture.
4. Pour batter into well greased cake tube pan.
5. Bake for 1 hour at 325°.
6. Frost with your favorite frosting, if desired.

UPSIDE-DOWN MANGO CAKE

(Mrs. Edward Schlesinger)

Mango Mix:
¼ cup butter
9 slices mango (approx.)
⅔ cup brown sugar

Cherries (pitted but can be fresh or canned).

1. Melt butter in 8 inch square pan. Add brown sugar.
2. Arrange mango slices over this and put cherries in between slices.
3. Pour Hot Water Sponge Cake Mix over this.
4. Bake one hour at 325°. Invert pan to cool.
5. Can be topped with whipped cream when served.

Hot Water Sponge Cake:
2 eggs
¼ cup boiling water
⅛ teaspoon salt
½ teaspoon vanilla or almond extract

⅔ cup sugar
⅔ cup flour
½ teaspoon baking powder

1. Separate eggs. Beat yolks until very thick.
2. Gradually add sugar to yolks and mix well.
3. Add water, mix well then add flour, baking powder, salt and extract. Mix well.
4. Beat egg whites until stiff. Fold into flour mix.
5. Pour over mango mix.
6. Bake for 1 hour at 325°.
7. Invert pan to cool.

NOTE: Ceylon peach may also be used instead of mango.

COURTING CAKE

(Mrs. Wm. G. Hardy)

1 baked pastry pie shell   1 cup tart jelly
½ of your favorite cake recipe

1. In baked pie shell, put tart jelly and cover shell completely.
2. Make ½ your favorite cake recipe and pour batter over jelly.
3. Put in oven for 20-30 minutes at 375° (or length of time required in your recipe for the cake to bake).
4. Cool before cutting.

CEYLON PEACH MERINGUE CAKE

(Mrs. Alfred J. Beck)

½ cup butter   4 tablespoons milk
½ cup sugar   1 teaspoon baking powder
4 egg yolks   2 tablespoons cake flour
½ cup cake flour   ¼ teaspoon salt

1. Cream butter and sugar together, separate eggs. Beat yolks until thick, add to sugar mixture. Stir well.
2. Sift flour and measure. Add flour and milk. Sift 2 tablespoons flour with baking powder and salt. Add. Mix well.
3. Pour into two 8 inch layer cake pans. Add meringue topping.

Topping:

4 egg whites   1 teaspoon vanilla
¾ cup sugar   ¾ cup chopped nut meats

1. Beat egg whites to a froth. Sift sugar, gradually add to egg whites, beating constantly. Add vanilla. When whites peak, stop beating.
2. Spread topping on each of uncooked layers. Sprinkle chopped nuts on top of meringue.
3. Bake for 25 minutes at 350°. Allow to cool away from draft.

Filling:

1 cup whipping cream   1½ tablespoons powdered sugar
½ teaspoon vanilla
2 cups sliced Ceylon peaches
(or any freestone)

1. Whip the cream, add sugar, vanilla, mix well. Add peaches.
2. Put one layer meringue side down on cake plate. Spread filling on layer. Put second layer on top of filling with meringue side up.
3. Slice gently — store in refrigerator.

OLD WORLD CHEESE CAKE

(Mr. Newall F. Miller)

21 graham crackers (or vanilla
    wafers)
3 large packages Philadelphia
    brand cream cheese
½ cup sugar
1 pint sour cream
1 teaspoon vanilla

½ teaspoon salt
¼ pound (1 stick) butter
3 eggs
1 pint small curd creamed
    cottage cheese
2 tablespoons sugar

1. Make graham cracker crust: Roll graham crackers to fine powder and add 1 teaspoon sugar and ¼ pound melted butter.
2. Press crust into spring-form angel food cake pan 9½x4 inch. Save ¼ cup of crust crumbs for topping.
3. Cake: Mix cream cheese and cottage cheese together.
4. Add ½ cup sugar and salt to cheese.
5. Add eggs one at a time mixing thoroughly and slowly before adding next egg. Add vanilla. Let mixture stand until air is gone.
6. Pour batter into crust and bake 25 minutes at 375°.
7. Remove from oven. Mix 2 tablespoons sugar into sour cream and pour over cake. Sprinkle graham crumbs over top.
8. Return to oven and bake 5 minutes longer.
9. Turn off oven, open oven door and let cake cool in oven.
10. When cake is cool, remove from pan, put on dish. Chill in refrigerator until ready to serve.

ANGEL FOOD CAKE

(Miss Emma Nelson)

1½ cups egg whites
1 cup flour
1 teaspoon vanilla

1½ cups sugar
1 teaspoon cream of tartar

1. Sift flour before measuring, sift sugar before measuring.
2. Sift flour with ½ cup sugar three times.
3. Add cream of tartar to egg whites and beat until peaks. Add rest of sugar beating until glossy.
4. Fold egg whites into flour mix. Add vanilla.
5. Pour into ungreased angel food cake tin. Bang pan on counter to remove large air pockets.
6. Bake for 1 hour at 325°. Remove from oven and cool upside down on cake rack. When cool, remove pan.

WHITE CAKE WITH MOCHA FROSTING

(Mrs. M. A. Hortt)

1 cup sugar
2/3 cup milk
3 level teaspoons baking powder

1/2 cup butter
2 cups fine cake flour
1 teaspoon vanilla
3 egg whites

1. Cream the butter, sugar well.
2. Sift the flour and baking powder.
3. Add half milk and the vanilla to butter mix, beat, add half flour, mix well. Add balance of milk and balance of flour.
4. Beat egg whites until stiff. Fold into flour mixture.
5. Pour into greased pans (two 9 inch layer pans or long cake pan or square cake pan). Bake 35-45 minutes at 350°.

Mocha Frosting:
2 cups confectioners sugar
1 teaspoon vanilla
Cream

1/3 cup butter
1 1/2 teaspoon strong coffee

1. Cream butter and sugar.
2. Add coffee and vanilla. Mix well. Add enough cream, 1 tablespoon at time to make it spread easily.
3. Spread on top and sides of cake.

NOTE: Delicious variation: Cut cake into small squares. Frost top and sides of each square. In bowl put finely chopped peanuts. Put frosted square into bowl and cover with ground nuts. Remove to platter and continue until all little squares are covered.

SWEDISH ORANGE CAKE

(Mrs. August Burghard)

1/2 cup butter
2 eggs
2 cups flour
1 cup raisins
1 cup sugar plus 1/2 cup

1 cup sour milk
1/2 teaspoon soda
Juice and rind of one orange
1/2 teaspoon baking powder

1. Grate orange rind and put aside. Juice the orange and add 1/2 cup sugar, stir and let stand.
2. Cream butter and sugar. Add eggs. Mix well.
3. Put soda in sour milk and add to egg mix.
4. Sift flour and baking powder together then add to mix. Add raisins, orange rind.
5. Pour into long flat cake pan. Bake 45 minutes at 350°.
6. Remove from oven and pour orange juice mix over top.

DEVIL FOOD CAKE

(Mrs. H. D. Dichtenmueller,
1924 Woman's Club Cook Book)

¾ cup bitter chocolate
1½ cups sugar
3 eggs
2 cups cake flour

1½ cups milk
½ cup butter
1 teaspoon vanilla
1 teaspoon baking soda

1. In saucepan mix chocolate and ½ cup milk. Bring to boil and cook until smooth.
2. Cream sugar and butter. Add melted chocolate mixture.
3. Separate eggs. Beat yolks into chocolate mixture.
4. Add 1 cup milk alternately with flour. Dissolve soda in 1 tablespoon warm water. Add to flour mixture. Add vanilla.
5. Beat egg whites until stiff. Fold into flour mixture.
6. Pour batter into shallow cake pan or two layer pans which have been well greased.
7. Bake at 350°. Bake the layers about 30 minutes. Bake the shallow cake pan for about 45 minutes.

SCRIPTURE CAKE

(Mrs. Robert S. Pendleton)

4½ cups flour
1 cup butter
2 cups sugar
2 cups raisins
2 cups figs
2 teaspoons baking powder
2 cups almonds
2 tablespoons honey
1 pinch salt
6 eggs
½ cup milk

I Kings 4:22
Judges 5:25
Jeremiah 6:20
I Samuel 30:12
Nahum 3:12
Amos 4:5
Numbers 17:8
Samuel 14:25
Leviticus 2:13
Jeremiah 17:11
Judges 4:19

If you mix verse of I Kings with phrase in Judges, a word in Jeremiah and a pinch of Leviticus, you will have the basis for a real Christmas delicacy, namely Scripture Cake, King James Version. Follow the directions of Solomon for bringing up a child, Proverbs 23:14 "beat him with a rod." Bake in loaf pans for 50 minutes at 325°.

RUSSIAN RUM CAKE

(Mrs. Magnus Loftstedt)

Rum Cake:

1 baked sponge cake (plain   ½ cup water
   sponge in square tin)   ½ cup sugar
1 tablespoon rum

1. Mix sugar and water and boil for 5 minutes. Add rum. .
2. Sprinkle this mixture over the sponge cake carefully, not using any more than the cake can take.

Rum Cake Frosting:

1 cup unsalted butter   5 egg yolks
½ cup lukewarm strong coffee   ½ pound confectioners sugar

1. Cream butter thoroughly. Mix sugar and egg yolks. Add to butter.
2. Mix coffee in very slowly until frosting is of spreading consistency.
3. Spread thickly over Rum Cake. Enough for between layers, top and sides of cake.

ORANGE DATE CAKE

(Mrs. Robert S. Pendleton)

¾ cup shortening   1 cup sugar
1½ teaspoons vanilla   3 eggs
3 cups sifted flour   1½ teaspoons salt
¼ cup orange juice   ½ cup evaporated milk
2 cups pitted dates cut up   1 cup chopped pecan meats
Grated rind of one orange

1. Cream shortening, sugar and vanilla. Add eggs one at a time and mix well.
2. Sift the flour, soda and salt. Add to egg mix.
3. Add orange juice and evaporated milk. Fold in the rind, dates and nut meats.
4. Pour into greased pan and bake at 325° for 1½ hours.
5. Top with: ½ cup sugar, juice of 2 oranges and some grated rind, mix well. Pour this over the hot cake.
6. Cool cake and refrigerate at least 24 hours before using.

NOTE: A good party cake or use in place of fruit cake at Thanksgiving or Christmas.

DANISH CHRISTMAS CAKE

(Mrs. Donald C. Little)

2 cups scalded milk
¾ cup sugar
¼ cup lukewarm water
3 eggs
2 egg yolks
¾ pound seedless raisins

½ cup butter
2 yeast cakes
6 cups flour
¼ pound citron, sliced thin
1 tablespoon cardamon seed

1. Mix butter and sugar, add hot milk. Cool to lukewarm.
2. Crumble yeast into lukewarm water. Add to milk mixture. Beat in 2 cups flour. Add all eggs and the 2 egg yolks. Cover dish and set in warm place until double in bulk (1 hour).
3. Beat down dough. Add 4 cups flour, citron, raisins and seed. Knead. Shape into loaf shape and put into greased pans.
4. Cover and set in warm place to rise (let double in bulk).
5. Bake for 1 hour at 375°. Remove from oven and brush top with melted butter and let cool.

RED VELVET CAKE

(Mrs. Welcom H. Watson)

½ cup butter
2 ounces red cake coloring
1 teaspoon soda
1 teaspoon salt
1¼ cups cake flour

1½ cups sugar
2 eggs
2 tablespoons cocoa
1 cup buttermilk
1 teaspoon vinegar

1. Cream butter and sugar together. Add eggs. Add coloring.
2. Sift together flour, cocoa, and salt. Add to creamed mixture.
3. Add buttermilk. Mix.
4. Mix soda and vinegar together. Fold gently into cake mix.
5. Pour gently into three 8 inch cake pans and bake for 30-35 minutes at 350°.
6. Frost with Layer Cake Frosting.

APPLESAUCE CAKE

(Mrs. Robert S. Pendleton)

2½ cups unsweetened hot
    applesauce
1 cup shortening
1 teaspoon cinnamon
¼ teaspoon cloves
½ cup nut meats

2 cups sugar
2½ cups flour
½ teaspoon nutmeg
½ cup raisins
4 teaspoons baking soda

1. Mix sugar, flour, soda, cinnamon, nutmeg, cloves, add shortening and applesauce. Mix well. Add raisins and nuts.
2. Bake in greased cake pan for 1 hour at 375°.
3. Frost with Cooked Frosting.

COCONUT PINEAPPLE CAKE

(Mrs. Frank Stranahan)

1 layer cake which has been
    baked in three layers

Coconut icing
Pineapple marmalade

1. Spread pineapple marmalade between bottom and middle layers of cake.
2. Frost sides and top with icing.
3. Press grated coconut over sides and top of cake making coconut on top at least ½ inch thick.

NOTE: A real party cake!

GEORGIA 1-2-3-4 CAKE

(Mrs. Wm. H. Marshall)

1 cup butter
2 cups sugar
3 cups flour
4 eggs

1 cup milk (or water)
2 teaspoons baking powder
½ teaspoon lemon extract

1. Separate eggs. Slightly beat yolks. Add sugar and butter, cream well. Add egg yolks.
2. Sift flour and baking powder. Add flour and milk alternately to creamed sugar-butter mix. Add extract.
3. Beat egg whites until stiff. Fold into flour mixture.
4. Pour into well greased loaf pan.
5. Bake for 1¼ hours at 300°.

DATE AND NUT TORTE

(Miss Nola G. Bates)

4 eggs
1 cup raw sugar
1 teaspoon baking powder
½ cup filberts

¾ cup sifted flour
1 cup dates, pitted and cut
½ cup pecans
1 teaspoon vanilla

1. Beat eggs until very light. Add sugar gradually.
2. Sift flour with baking powder. Add to sugar mixture. Add vanilla, dates and nuts.
3. Pour into well greased 8 inch pan.
4. Bake at 350° for about 40 minutes. Cool.
5. Cut into strips and top with either ice cream or whipped cream.

JAEGER TORTE

(Mrs. David B. Gilliam)

½ pound powdered sugar
8 eggs

½ pound ground almonds

1. Separate eggs. Beat sugar and egg yolks for 15 minutes (electric beater at medium for 5 minutes).
2. Add almonds and mix well.
3. Stiffly beat egg whites. Add to almond mixture.
4. Bake 50 minutes at 350° in ungreased tube cake pan.
5. When done, turn upside down and cool for one hour before removing from pan.
6. Frost with Chocolate Icing.

Chocolate Icing:

1 whole cake German chocolate
6 tablespoons powdered sugar
2 egg whites

1 tablespoon butter
1 teaspoon vanilla

1. Melt chocolate and butter in double boiler.
2. Beat egg whites until stiff, add sugar.
3. Fold egg whites into chocolate, add vanilla, spread on cake.

SOPA BORRACHA

(Recipe Selection Committee)

1 stale pound cake
Sweet wine

Cinnamon

1. Put cake in bowl, or pan. Pour sweet wine over cake soaking entirely. Stop pouring when cake will no longer absorb wine.
2. To serve, slice and put on plate. Sprinkle with cinnamon.

BOB'S FAVORITE COOKIES

(Mrs. Alfred J. Beck)

1 cup melted butter
2 eggs
¼ teaspoon salt
1 teaspoon soda

1 pound brown sugar
1 cup ground pecans
1 teaspoon vanilla
5 to 5½ cups cake flour

1. Break eggs into bowl, beat slightly. Add brown sugar, butter, salt, soda, vanilla and pecans. Mix well.
2. Add flour to mixture.
3. Line 6½x10½ inch pan with waxed paper. Pack cookie dough firmly into pan and refrigerate overnight.
4. Cut dough in half the long way, then thinly slice each half.
5. Bake on ungreased cookie sheet at 350° for 8 to 10 minutes. Watch so cookie does not brown too much or burn.
6. Can be stored in a tin.

BROWNIES

(Mrs. D. G. Lawrence)

½ cup butter
2 cups nuts
2 squares baking chocolate
¼ teaspoon salt

1 cup sugar
2 eggs
1 teaspoon vanilla
½ cup flour

1. Cream butter, sugar. Beat in eggs.
2. Melt chocolate and add to egg mixture. Add flour, salt, vanilla. Stir well. Add nuts.
3. Bake in greased pan for 35 minutes at 350°

OATMEAL COOKIES

(Mrs. Earl J. Meiers)

¾ cup shortening
½ cup granulated sugar
¼ cup water
1 cup flour
½ teaspoon soda
1 cup brown sugar

1 egg
1 teaspoon vanilla
1 teaspoon salt
3 cups uncooked oats
½ cup raisins

1. Mix shortening, sugar, egg, water, vanilla. Beat.
2. Sift flour, salt and soda. Add to shortening mixture.
3. Mix oats and raisins. Mix well.
4. Drop on greased cookie sheet.
5. Bake at 350° for about 15 minutes.

MOLASSES DROP COOKIES (2 dozen)

(Mrs. Tom G. Lively)

4 tablespoons butter
⅓ cup sugar
1 egg
1¾ cups flour
⅓ cup molasses
¼ cup hot water

½ teaspoon salt
1 teaspoon ginger
½ teaspoon cinnamon
1 teaspoon soda
¼ teaspoon baking powder

1. Cream butter and sugar together. Beat egg and add. Add molasses.
2. Sift flour, salt, ginger, cinnamon, baking powder together.
3. Add soda to hot water. Add to molasses mixture.
4. Add flour to molasses mixture, stirring well.
5. Drop from teaspoon onto greased cookie sheet.
6. Bake 10-12 minutes at 400°.

NOTE: This is medium hard cookie.

CHEESE COOKIES

(Miss Nola G. Bates)

2 cups bread flour
½ cup butter
Sesame or poppy seeds

1¼ teaspoons salt
½ pound (2 cups) American cheese

1. Sift flour with salt. Cut in butter. Grate cheese and cut into flour.
2. Chill dough for several hours. Roll out very thin. Cut in small rounds. Sprinkle tops with seeds.
3. Bake at 450° for 10 minutes.

NOTE: Stores well in tightly covered jar.

30 MINUTE BUTTER COOKIES (about 20 cookies)

(Mrs. Wm. H. Marshall)

6 tablespoons butter
1 well beaten egg yolk
1 cup sifted all purpose flour

6 tablespoons powdered sugar
1 teaspoon vanilla
Whole nut meats (20)

1. Cream butter and sugar. Add egg yolk, vanilla. Add flour. Mix well.
2. Drop by teaspoonful onto ungreased cookie sheet.
3. Bake 15 to 20 minutes at 350°. Remove from oven.
4. While still hot, press whole nut meat into center of each cookie.

ORANGE COOKIE

(Woman's Club Section, Ft. Lauderdale Sentinel, March 14, 1924)

½ cup butter
1 egg
Grated rind of 1 orange
2 cups flour

1 cup sugar
1 teaspoon baking powder
½ cup orange juice

1. Cream butter and sugar. Slightly beat egg. Add to butter mixture. Add rind and orange juice. Mix well.
2. Put baking powder into flour. Sift. Add to orange mixture.
3. Drop by teaspoonful onto greased baking sheet. Press to flatten cookie.
4. Bake about 15 minutes at 350°.

MEDALLIONS

(Mrs. Donald C. Little)

1 cup shortening
3 eggs

1 cup sugar
2 cups flour

1. Mix sugar and shortening. Add eggs, then mix flour in well.
2. Roll out. Cut with cookie cutter. Count cookies and in one-half the number punch out small hole in middle.
3. Bake on cookie sheet for 15 minutes at 350°. Cool.
4. On solid cookie spread tart jelly. Put cookie with hole on top. Dribble Sugar Water Icing on top.

CHRISTMAS FRUIT BAR

(Mrs. Welcom H. Watson)

2 cups pecans
1 stick butter
1 teaspoon vanilla
5 rounds of candied pineapple

½ box light brown sugar
2 eggs
1 cup flour
½ pound candied cherries

1. Cream butter and sugar. Add eggs, flour and vanilla.
2. Grease and flour flat pan. Sprinkle chopped nuts on bottom of pan. (13x8 inch best size).
3. Pour batter into pan. Sprinkle cut up pineapple and cherries on top of batter.
4. Bake for one hour at 300°. Remove from oven.
5. Cut into 36 bars at once.

CHOCOLATE MARSHMALLOW DROPS (4 dozen)

(Mrs. Robert S. Pendleton)

1¾ cups sifted flour
½ teaspoon salt
½ cup soft shortening
1 egg, beaten
½ cup milk
24 large marshmallows

½ teaspoon baking soda
½ cup cocoa
1 cup sugar
1 teaspoon vanilla
½ cup chopped walnuts

1. Sift flour with baking soda, salt, cocoa. Mix shortening, sugar, egg, vanilla until creamy, add milk. Mix into flour mixture blending well after each addition. Add nuts.
2. Drop by teaspoonful onto well greased cookie sheet.
3. Bake about 8 minutes at 375°.
4. Using floured scissors, cut marshmallows horizontally. Place half marshmallow, cut side down on each hot cookie.
5. Return to oven for 4 minutes. Remove and cool. Spread with Cocoa Glaze.

HERMITS

(Mrs. John T. Schroeder, 1924
Woman's Club Cook Book)

2 cups brown sugar
2 cups raisins
1 cup nuts
1 teaspoon soda
1 teaspoon nutmeg
1 teaspoon cinnamon

1 cup butter
1 cup currants
3 eggs
3 tablespoons sour milk
1 teaspoon cloves
3½ cups sifted flour

1. Cream sugar and butter. Add eggs, mix well.
2. Drop raisins, currants in flour. Remove. Add soda to buttermilk. Add nutmeg, cinnamon, cloves to flour.
3. Add milk to butter mixture. Add flour to butter mixture. Mix well.
4. Add raisins, currants and nuts to batter.
5. Drop by spoonful onto greased cookie pan.
6. Bake 15-18 minutes at 375°.

SAND TARTS

(Mrs. Kenneth Richardson,
1924 Woman's Club Cook Book)

½ cup butter
1 egg
2 teaspoons baking powder

1 cup sugar
1¾ cups flour

1. Cream butter, sugar and egg. Mix in flour and baking powder.
2. Chill dough (at least one hour, more if desired).
3. Roll dough very thin. Cut out cookies.
4. Place cookies on greased cookie tin and sprinkle with granulated sugar.
5. Bake 8 minutes at 350°.

DATE NUT BALLS

(Mrs. Walter B. Hilliard)

1 8 ounce package pitted dates
1 beaten egg
2½ cups crisp rice cereal
1 teaspoon vanilla
1 cup granulated sugar

½ cup butter
½ cup chopped nuts
1 cup shredded coconut (or enough to roll balls in)

1. Cut up dates. Place dates, sugar, egg, butter in saucepan over moderate heat. Bring to boil and boil for 10 minutes stirring constantly.
2. Remove from heat and partially cool.
3. Add rice cereal, nuts and vanilla. Mix well.
4. Form into balls about the size of a walnut.
5. Roll in shredded coconut. Makes about 40 cookies.

NOTE: Delicious and easy to make.

CRANBERRY CRUNCH

(Mrs. C. W. Schlueter)

1 cup quick cooking rolled oats
½ cup sifted flour
½ cup butter
1 tablespoon lemon juice

¾ cup brown sugar
½ cup moist shredded coconut
1 can (1 pound size) whole cranberry sauce

1. Mix oats, brown sugar, flour and coconut. Cut in butter until crumbly.
2. Put half the mixture into a greased baking dish (8x8x2 inch size).
3. Combine cranberry sauce and lemon juice. Spread on top of batter. Put remaining batter on top of cranberries.
4. Bake for 40 minutes at 350°. While hot cut into squares. Put vanilla ice cream on top, serve at once.

ORANGE GLAZE

(Mrs. Mary Tsolas)

2 tablespoons orange juice   1 teaspoon butter
1 cup confectioners sugar

1. Heat orange juice. Add butter, mix well. Remove from heat.
2. Stir in sugar. Blend well.

~~~~~~~~~~~~~~~~~~~~~~~~~

COCOA GLAZE

(Mrs. Robert S. Pendleton)

2 cups confectioners sugar   ½ cup cocoa
4-6 tablespoons hot milk

1. Mix sugar and cocoa. Add 4 tablespoons hot milk and mix well. If too stiff add a little more milk. Should be soft enough to spread easily.

~~~~~~~~~~~~~~~~~~~~~~~~~

TART LEMON FILLING (for a 2-layer cake)

(Mrs. Magnus Loftstedt)

1 cup sugar   1 egg
1 lemon, juice and grated rind   1 tablespoon butter
1 grated apple

1. In saucepan mix sugar, egg, lemon juice, rind and apple.
2. Cook for 5 to 7 minutes. Remove from heat, add butter.
3. Cool. Use between layers of cake.

~~~~~~~~~~~~~~~~~~~~~~~~~

COOKED FROSTING

(Mrs. Robert S. Pendleton)

2 cups sugar   ⅔ cup cream
1 tablespoon butter   1 teaspoon vanilla

1. Mix all ingredients in saucepan. Cook on low fire until well blended. Remove from fire and cool.
2. Beat well.

SUGAR WATER ICING

(Mrs. Donald C. Little)

2 tablespoons water   1 cup confectioners sugar
¼ teaspoon vanilla

1. Mix sugar, water and vanilla. If too stiff, add a little more water.
2. This should be spread on cake, cookies, doughnuts while they are still warm.

CHOCOLATE FROSTING

(Mrs. H. D. Dichtenmueller,
1924 Woman's Club Cook Book)

1 cup bitter chocolate   ½ cup condensed milk
1 egg yolk   Dash salt
1 teaspoon butter   Confectioners sugar
Nuts if desired   ½ teaspoon vanilla

1. In saucepan mix chocolate and condensed milk. Boil until thick. Remove from fire. Quickly stir in egg yolk and dash of salt. Add butter. Stir well.
2. If frosting is too thin, add 1 tablespoon confectioners sugar, mix well. Continue until it is right consistency to spread.
3. Beat well. Add vanilla. Beat. Mix in nuts if desired, or frost cake and sprinkle nuts on frosting.

LAYER CAKE FROSTING

(Mrs. Wm. G. Crawford)

11 tablespoons cake flour   1¼ cups sweet milk
 1 cup sugar   1 cup butter
 1 teaspoon vanilla

1. Mix flour and milk. Cook over low heat. Stir until thick. Remove from heat.
2. Beat sugar and butter into mixture. Add vanilla. Continue beating until fluffy.

INLAND WATERWAY, FORT LAUDERDALE, FLORIDA

Confections

Sweets to the sweet . . . .

Hamlet
William Shakespeare
(1564-1616)

PANOCHE

(Mrs. Harriett S. Hector,
1917 So. Methodist Cook Book)

3 cups brown sugar
2 tablespoons butter
1 teaspoon vanilla

1 can evaporated milk
1 cup chopped nut meats

1. Mix sugar, milk, butter in saucepan and bring to boil.
2. Boil until soft ball stage. Remove from heat.
3. Beat until mixture becomes thick.
4. Add nuts and vanilla.
5. Pour into well greased pan to cool.

PINEAPPLE FUDGE

(Mrs. Wm. E. Lemkau)

2 cups sugar
½ cup pineapple, crushed
and well drained

½ cup cream
1 tablespoon butter
½ cup nut meats (if desired)

1. Mix sugar, cream, pineapple and cook until soft ball stage is reached. Remove from fire.
2. Add butter and nuts, mix well. Allow to cool.
3. Beat until creamy then pour onto buttered platter.
4. Cut into 1 inch squares.

PRALINES

(Mrs. James F. Smalley)

2 cups white sugar
⅔ cup milk
⅛ teaspoon soda
2 cups pecans

¼ cup butter (1 stick)
1 teaspoon salt
1 teaspoon vanilla

1. In saucepan, mix sugar, milk, salt, butter, soda. Stir well. Bring mixture to boil. Cook to soft ball stage.
2. Add vanilla and pecans. Beat until stiff.
3. Drop from spoon onto waxed paper or well buttered dish.

DIVINITY FUDGE

(Mrs. C. E. Brinson,
1924 Woman's Club Cook Book)

3 cups sugar
⅓ cup White Karo Syrup
Nuts, raisins or candied cherries

⅔ cup water
2 egg whites

1. Mix sugar, syrup, water in sauce pan.
2. Boil slowly without stirring until liquid spins a thread from a spoon.
3. Beat egg whites until stiff.
4. Pour boiling liquid slowly into egg whites, beating whites fast then more slowly, until mixture begins to thicken.
5. Drop from spoon onto buttered dish.
6. Nuts, raisins or candied cherries may be added while beating if desired.

ORANGE FUDGE

(Mrs. Wm. E. Lemkau)

Juice of one orange
¼ teaspoon soda
Grated rind of orange

3 cups sugar
3 tablespoons butter
Milk

1. Juice one orange and put juice through strainer to remove any seeds, pulp. Put juice in measuring cup. Add soda. Add enough milk to orange juice to fill cup to ¾ mark.
2. Put into saucepan, sugar and orange juice mix. Bring to boil. When soft ball stage is reached remove from fire. Add butter and rind. Cool.
3. When cool, beat until creamy. Pour onto buttered dish and score into pieces.

PECAN KISSES

(Mrs. W. T. Crawford)

1 cup brown sugar
1 cup pecan halves

1 egg white

1. Beat egg white until stiff. Beat in sugar. Add pecans.
2. Drop by teaspoonful onto cookie sheet.
3. Bake for 25 minutes at 300°.

MOLASSES POPCORN BALLS

(Recipe Selection Committee)

6 cups popped corn
⅓ cup molasses
¾ cup sugar
¼ cup water

1 tablespoon vinegar
¼ teaspoon salt
1½ tablespoons butter

1. In saucepan put molasses, sugar, water, vinegar and salt. Cook slowly without stirring until temperature reaches 270° or threads in cup cold water.
2. Remove from heat and add butter. Stir enough to mix in butter.
3. Pour over popped corn and form into balls.

COCONUT CRUNCH

(Mrs. Tom G. Lively)

1. Open fresh coconut and cut out meat.
2. Using potato peeler, shred coconut into thin strips.
3. Butter cookie sheet.
4. Place one layer of shredded coconut on cookie sheet. Sprinkle lightly with sugar.
5. Place in 350° oven for approx. 15-20 minutes, or until coconut is brown.

NOTE: This may be eaten as is or may be crumbled for topping on cakes, cookies, ice cream, etc.

TOASTED SALTED NUT MEATS

(Recipe Selection Committee)

1. Heat ½ cup salad oil or butter in frying pan. Add about 1 cup nut meats. Cook until brown stirring constantly.
2. Remove nuts from oil and put on paper towel to drain. Sprinkle with salt.
3. Add another cup of nuts to oil in pan and follow same procedure. Add more oil if necessary.

MOTHER'S SUGARED NUTS

(Mrs. Welcom H. Watson)

2 cups sugar
½ tablespoon salt
1 teaspoon vanilla

½ cup cream
¼ teaspoon cream tartar
4 cups pecans

1. In pan mix sugar, cream, salt and cream tartar. Boil until medium soft ball forms in water. Remove from heat.
2. Add vanilla and nuts to mixture, stir.
3. Drop on oiled paper or greased dish.

CRYSTALLIZED GRAPEFRUIT PEEL

(Recipe Selection Committee)

1. Wash fruit carefully. Rinse well. Cut peel off fruit then cut into small strips about 1 x ¼ inches wide.
2. Put two cups peel in pot, add about 6 cups water and bring to boil. Boil 10 minutes. Drain.
3. Repeat step No. 2 for at least 3 times or until the bitter flavor leaves the peel. Cool.
4. Weigh peel. For each ¼ pound of peel add ½ cup sugar and ¼ cup water. Boil. Continue to boil until syrup is absorbed. Remove from heat.
5. In paper bag put some sugar. Drop small amount of peel into bag and shake. Remove from bag and add more peel.
6. Put peel on flat sheet for about one hour. Can be stored. Put wax paper between layers of fruit.

NOTE: Same instructions for orange peel, lime peel and lemon peel.

CANDIED PINEAPPLE CHIPS

(1917 So. Methodist Cook Book)

1. Peel pineapple, removing eyes and cut into thin strips.
2. Lay on platter and cover with granulated sugar, keeping pieces separated and in a single layer.
3. Each day drain off juice which has accumulated (this may be saved and used). Turn pieces, re-sugar.
4. When no more juice accumulates and pineapple is dry, it may be packed into a container for storage. Put in a single layer on waxed paper and put on lid. May be stored in cool dry place.

TRAVELER'S PALM TREE, FORT LAUDERDALE, FLORIDA

Desserts and Sauces

The proof of the pudding is in the eating.

Don Quixote
Miguel de Cervantes
(1547-1616)

POMPADOUR PUDDING

(Miss Nola G. Bates)

1 quart milk	3 eggs
1½ cups sugar	3½ tablespoons corn starch
Dash salt	1 teaspoon vanilla
⅛ pound (2 ounces) chocolate	2 tablespoons milk

1. In saucepan put milk, cornstarch, salt, and ¾ cup of sugar. Separate eggs. Put yolks in milk mixture. Cook over low heat stirring constantly until smooth and thick. Remove from heat. Stir in vanilla.
2. Pour into custard cups, filling ⅔ full.
3. Make Chocolate Covering and pour over custard.
4. Bake at 350 until chocolate puffs and starts to crack, or about 30 minutes. Chill and serve.

Chocolate Covering:
1. In saucepan melt chocolate, ¾ cup sugar and 2 tablespoons of milk. Beat egg whites until stiff and fold into chocolate.
2. Pour over custard in cups and bake as above.

STRAWBERRY CHARLOTTE

(Mrs. Alfred J. Beck)

1 pint milk	1 tablespoon unflavored
2 tablespoons cornstarch	gelatine
½ cup sugar	2 tablespoons cold water
2 egg yolks	½ pint cream
1½ dozen lady fingers (approx.)	1 pint fresh strawberries

1. Heat milk in double boiler. Add cornstarch and sugar. Cook until thick, stirring constantly.
2. Beat egg yolks. Add to milk mixture and cook a few minutes longer.
3. Add gelatine to cold water, when soft add to milk mixture. Stir well and let cool.
4. When thick, whip cream and fold whipped cream into gelatine mixture.
5. Line bottom of mold with waxed paper. Cut one end off lady fingers. Stand long pieces around sides of mold and arrange small pieces on bottom along side long pieces. Pour half gelatine mixture into mold. Put in sliced or whole berries. Pour in rest of gelatine mixture. When stiff, unmold.

BERRY BREAD PUDDING

(Mrs. Phoebe N. Conklin)

1¾ cups scalded milk
½ teaspoon salt
½ teaspoon lemon extract
2 cups bread cubes

¼ cup honey
½ teaspoon vanilla
2 eggs beaten
1 cup berries

1. Place all ingredients in bowl and mix lightly.
2. Pour into 2 quart greased casserole.
3. Bake about 25 minutes at 350 .
4. Serve warm or cold with cream or sauce.

BERRY PUFF (serves 6)

(U. of Fla. Agr. Ext. Service
Circular 167)

2½ cups berries (canned or
   frozen)
½ cup sugar
¼ teaspoon cream of tartar
2 tablespoons cake flour

2 eggs, separated
½ cup juice from berries
2 tablespoons quick cooking
   tapioca
⅓ cup sugar

1. Crush berries. Add juice and ½ cup sugar. Stir in tapioca. Bring to boil, reduce heat and simmer 5 minutes stirring constantly.
2. Beat egg whites until foamy. Add salt and cream of tartar. Beat until stiff but not dry. Beat yolks until thick. Add sugar to yolks and beat. Fold whites into yolks and add flour.
3. Put berry mixture into casserole (1½ quart). Cover with egg mixture.
4. Bake 40 minutes at 325 . Serve warm.

1-2-3 PUDDING

(Mrs. Magnus Loftstedt)

1 cup brown sugar
2 cups milk

3 tablespoons minute tapioca
1 teaspoon vanilla

1. Mix all ingredients together.
2. Pour into greased baking pan. Place pan in dish of hot water.
3. Bake for 45 minutes at 350 , stirring two or three times while baking.
4. May be served either hot or cold with cream.

LEMON SPONGE PUDDING (serves 4 to 6)

(Mrs. Mary H. Walker)

2 eggs
1 cup sugar
⅛ teaspoon salt
Juice of one lemon (or lime)

1 cup milk
⅓ cup flour
1 teaspoon butter
Grated rind of lemon (or lime)

1. Separate eggs. Beat yolks until thick.
2. Heat milk, add butter.
3. Pour heated milk mixture over beaten egg yolks slowly and mix thoroughly.
4. Mix sugar, flour, salt. Stir in lemon juice and rind and add to yolk mixture.
5. Beat egg whites until stiff and fold into mixture.
6. Pour into buttered baking dish and put dish in pan of hot water.
7. Bake at 325° for 45 minutes.

GUAVA DUFF

(Recipe Selection Committee)

3 eggs
1 cup sugar
4 teaspoons baking powder
2 cups guava pulp

½ stick butter
3 cups flour
Dash salt

1. Slice fresh guavas thinly. Simmer in a little water for about 5 minutes. Push through sieve to make the pulp.
2. Cream butter, sugar. Beat eggs, add. Add guava pulp and mix thoroughly.
3. Add baking powder and salt to flour, beat constantly.
4. When mixture is thick pour into can (or pan with top) which has been lined with paper and greased. Immerse in kettle with water ⅔ way up can.
5. Steam for two hours. Slice and serve with egg sauce.

Egg Sauce:
Beat ½ cup sugar into 3 eggs. Keep beating until sugar completely dissolves. If not sweet enough, slowly add more sugar. Mix ¼ teaspoon vanilla in. Serve.

CHOCOLATE UPSIDE-DOWN PUDDING

(Mrs. Robert S. Pendleton)

¾ cup sugar
2 teaspoons baking powder
2 tablespoons butter
1 teaspoon vanilla
½ cup nuts
½ cup brown sugar
1 cup boiling water

1¼ cups sifted flour
¼ teaspoon salt
1 square unsweetened chocolate (1 ounce)
½ cup sugar
2 tablespoons cocoa
½ cup milk

1. Sift together the ¾ cup sugar, flour, baking powder and salt.
2. Melt together the butter, chocolate, add milk, vanilla, nuts.
3. Mix chocolate mix with flour mix.
4. Pour into well greased cake dish. Mix ½ cup white sugar with the brown sugar. Sprinkle over top of batter.
5. Mix cocoa in boiling water. Pour over top of batter.
6. Bake for 1 hour at 350°.

CUBAN FLAN (serves 10)

(Recipe Selection Committee)

1½ cups sugar
4 cups milk
1 teaspoon vanilla

8 eggs
1 stick cinnamon

1. In heavy saucepan, carmelize ½ cup sugar (stir dry in pan until melted and golden brown and it sticks to side of pan). Allow to cool.
2. Beat eggs until foamy, gradually add 1 cup sugar, beating well after each addition.
3. In separate pan heat milk with cinnamon stick (do not boil). Remove stick. Gradually add hot milk to egg mixture, stirring until sugar completely dissolves. Add vanilla.
4. Pour mixture into carmel-lined pan. Put pan in pan of hot water.
5. Bake at 350° for about 1 hour or until knife inserted comes out clean. Cool and serve.

HOT RICE PUDDING WITH CALICO SAUCE (serves 6)

(Mrs. Mary Ann May Wood)

½ cup chopped fresh strawberries

½ cup Hard Sauce
Favorite Rice Pudding

1. Mix Hard Sauce and strawberries. Put in refrigerator (or deep freeze) until very cold.
2. Make your favorite Rice Pudding.
3. To serve, place cold Hard Sauce on very hot Rice Pudding. Serve at once.

NOTE: See index for recipes of Hard Sauce and Brown's Old Fashioned Rice Pudding.

ZABAGLIONE (serves 6)

(Recipe Selection Committee)

6 egg yolks
Dash salt
Juice of lemon & grated rind

¾ cup sugar
⅔ cup sherry or Marsala wine

1. Mix yolks, sugar. Add salt, lemon juice, rind and wine.
2. In heavy bottom pot, heat mixture and beat with rotary beater until mixture is foamy and holds it shape.
3. Put into sherbert glasses. Serve warm or chill.

NOTE: This may also be served over cake or fruit.

BERRY PUDDING

(Mrs. Alvarez Stanford)

1 cup sugar
3 cups flour
1 tablespoon butter, melted
1 egg

1 teaspoon salt
2 heaping teaspoons baking powder
1 quart berries

1. Use about one cup of the flour to roll berries in.
2. In bowl beat egg. Add sugar, flour, butter, salt, baking powder. Mix well. Add berries.
3. Turn into well floured pudding bag.
4. Put bag into large kettle and cover with water. Boil for one hour, turning over once or twice.
5. Slice and serve with hard sauce.

NOTE: Mrs. Stanford's mother made this, buying her berries from the Indians when they came to town. If you don't have a pudding bag, use two layers of strong cheese cloth, tied securely.

MANGO CRISP

(Mrs. Henry O. Patton)

2 mangos (approx.) ripe
½ teaspoon cinnamon
1 cup flour

3 tablespoon brown sugar
½ teaspoon nutmeg
½ cup butter

1. Peel and slice mangos. Slice enough to cover bottom of wide shallow casserole dish. When through slicing, take seed in hand and squeeze juice over sliced fruit.
2. Mix brown sugar, nutmeg and cinnamon. Sprinkle mixture over mangos.
3. Mix flour with butter and sprinkle over mangos.
4. Bake for about 30 minutes at 350°
5. To serve, top with ice cream or whipped cream.

BROWN'S OLD FASHIONED RICE PUDDING

(Logan T. Brown by Homer C. Stuckey)

⅓ cup raw rice
¼ teaspoon salt
1 teaspoon vanilla
½ cup seedless raisins

⅓ cup sugar
1 quart whole milk
⅛ teaspoon nutmeg

1. Mix rice, sugar, salt, vanilla, sugar, nutmeg and milk.
2. Pour into baking dish.
3. Cook at 250 for 2 hours, stirring every 20 minutes. When rice has been cooking 1½ hours, add raisins.

MOCK INDIAN PUDDING (Cornflake Pudding)

(Mrs. Magnus Loftstedt)

3 cups cornflakes
2 eggs
⅓ cup molasses

3 cups milk
½ cup sugar
Dash salt

1. Beat eggs. Add milk, sugar, molasses and salt. Add cornflakes.
2. Pour into greased baking dish.
3. Bake for 45 minutes at 350°.

MOTHER'S 1874 SUET PUDDING

(Mrs. J. J. VanderVeer)

1½ cups chopped suet   1 cup molasses
1 cup sweet milk   1 cup raisins
1 cup currants   1 cup flour
¼ teaspoon cinnamon   ¼ teaspoon cloves
¼ teaspoon nutmeg   ¼ teaspoon ginger
1 teaspoon soda   1 tablespoon salt

1. Roll fruit in flour which has soda mix in. Add suet, milk, molasses, mix. Add spices, salt.
2. Put into greased mold (or 1 pound coffee can) and steam 4 to 5 hours. Cover with foil or waxed paper. Cool.
3. Remove from mold and store in refrigerator. Keep wrapped.
4. To use, reheat in top of double boiler for at least ¾ hour. Serve with hard sauce.

BERRIES WITH DUMPLINGS

(U. of Fla. Agr. Ext. Service
Circular 167)

1 cup flour   1 teaspoon baking powder
1 tablespoon sugar   ¼ teaspoon salt
2 tablespoons shortening   ¼ cup milk
3 cups fresh berries   ½ cup water
1 cup sugar   2 tablespoons butter

1. Mix flour, baking powder, sugar and salt. Melt shortening and add to milk. Blend into flour mixture.
2. In saucepan put berries, water, sugar and butter. Cover and bring to boil.
3. Drop dumplings by spoonful onto hot berries. Cover and cook 12-15 minutes.
4. Serve hot with cream.

MANGO PARFAIT (serves 8)

(Mrs. Henry O. Patton)

2 ripe mangos   1 quart peach ice cream

1. Peel mangos, slice, then puree. Put in refrigerator to chill.
2. In parfait dish put layer of peach ice cream and layer of mango puree. Continue layers until dish is full. Serve at once.

~~~~~~~~~~~~~~~~~~~~~~~~~

FRESH LIME SHERBERT (serves 6)

(Mrs. Mary Tsolas)

1 cup light corn syrup   1 cup sugar
3 cups water   ⅔ cup lime juice (Persian)
2 tablespoons grated lime peel   2 egg whites, beaten stiff
½ pint heavy cream, whipped thick

1. Combine corn syrup, sugar and water in sauce pan. Bring to boil, boil 5 minutes without stirring.
2. Cool, add lime juice and lime peel. Put in freezer.
3. When frozen, beat until mushy.
4. Fold in beaten egg whites and the whipped cream.
5. Return to freezer and freeze for at least 4 hours before serving.

NOTE: Key lime may be substituted for the Persian lime. Use ½ cup Key lime juice and 1 tablespoon of rind.

~~~~~~~~~~~~~~~~~~~~~~~~~

AVOCADO ICE CREAM

(1917 So. Methodist Cook Book)

6 egg yolks   1 quart milk
2 cups sugar   1 teaspoon vanilla
4 avocados boiled   ¼ teaspoon almond extract

1. Make boiled custard of yolks, milk and one cup sugar. When cooked, add vanilla.
2. Mash avocados with 1 cup sugar. Add almond extract.
3. When custard is cool, add avocado mix to it.
4. Freeze slowly.
5. Serve with slivered almonds and cherries.

HOMEMADE ICE CREAM

(Mrs. Ralph R. Lehr)

6 eggs
½ gallon whipping cream
2 tablespoons vanilla (or other flavoring)

2 cups sugar
1 quart whole milk

1. Break eggs into large bowl. Add sugar and beat until creamy. Add cream and flavoring. Mix well. Pour into one gallon freezer and fill to within 3 or 4 inches of top with the whole milk.
2. Place cover on can. Put into freezer bucket. Fill bucket with alternate layers of ⅔ ice and ⅓ ice cream salt. Freeze until stiff. Be sure to crush ice fine.)
3. Use instructions with freezer for mixing.

NOTE: This is a good vanilla ice cream. It is also the base for your fresh fruit ice creams.

BANANAS FLAMBEAU (serves 4)

(Recipe Selection Committee)

4 ripe but firm bananas
¼ cup brown sugar
¾ cup grated coconut

½ cup orange juice
2 tablespoons butter
4 ounces rum

1. Peel bananas. Slice in half lengthwise.
2. Mix orange juice and brown sugar and melted butter.
3. Using smallest flat dish the bananas fit into, place halved bananas in greased pan.
4. Pour orange juice mix over bananas. Cover top with coconut.
5. Bake for 15 minutes at 400° or until bananas are soft.
6. Heat rum. Pour over bananas and ignite. Serve at once.

LOQUAT DESSERT

(Broward County Home
Demonstration Agent)

Wash freshly picked fruit that is ripe but still firm. Remove blossom and stem end. Cut. Remove seed. Peel or leave skin on as you wish. Place in bowl and sprinkle with small amount of sugar. Chill. Serve with milk or cream.

BAKED AVOCADOS

(Recipe Selection Committee)

2 ripe but not soft avocados
Grated cheese
Garlic salt

2 cups diced shrimp or chicken
or ham in white sauce

1. Slice avocados in half. Remove seed. Put halves on cookie sheet.
2. Make favorite creamed meat or fish dish. Put creamed meat or fish in cavity of avocado.
3. Sprinke little garlic salt on top of each. Sprinkle little cheese (grated) on top of each.
4. Bake about 15 minutes at 375° or until cheese is melted and brown. Serve at once.

BAKED BANANAS (serves 4)

(Recipe Selection Committee)

4 firm bananas
4 tablespoons butter

1 cup orange juice
Sugar and cinnamon

1. Peel bananas. Slice in half length-wise. Put in buttered baking dish in single layer.
2. Break butter into bits and put on top bananas. Pour orange juice over bananas. Sprinkle tops with sugar and cinnamon.
3. Bake about 45 minutes at 350° or until juice in pan is a syrup.

BAKED PAPAYA (serves 4)

(Recipe Selection Committee)

2 firm papayas
2 tablespoons lime juice

1 stick butter
2 tablespoons candied ginger

1. In pan melt butter, add lime juice, cut candied ginger into bits and add to butter. Let mix stand for about 1 hour.
2. Cut papayas in half lengthwise. Scoop out seeds.
3. Put papaya in shallow baking dish which has been greased. Brush papaya with butter mix, pouring remainder into cavities.
4. Put in oven for 30 minutes at 350° or until fruit is tender. Brush fruit every five minutes with butter mix. Serve at once.

EGG FRUIT DESSERT (serves 4)

(Mrs. Sandie Marsh)

1 cup egg fruit flesh
1 tablespoon brown sugar
Dash cinnamon

1 tablespoon lime juice
1 tablespoon butter
Whipped cream

1. Peel egg fruit. Remove seeds. Lightly pack flesh in measuring cup. Fill to 1 cup level.
2. Mash egg fruit. Add lime juice, brown sugar, soft butter and dash cinnamon. Chill.
3. Whip cream. Put egg fruit mix in custard cup and top with whipped cream.

AMBROSIA

(Godey's Lady's Book, 1869)

1 cup grated fresh coconut   1 cup grated fresh pineapple

1. Put layer of pineapple in dish, sprinkle with sugar, put in layer of coconut, sprinkle with sugar. Continue until all coconut and pineapple used up.
2. Put in refrigerator for 2 - 3 hours before serving.

NOTE: Orange can be substituted for pineapple. Sugar may be omitted. Honey may be used instead of sugar.

GUAVA SHELLS AND CREAM CHEESE

(Recipe Selection Committee)

1 cup preserved guava shells   Salt crackers
1 package cream cheese

1. Chill guava shells. Put into sauce dish along with syrup. Cut cream cheese into strips and put one strip in each dish.
2. Serve with salt crackers.

CHOCOLATE SYRUP

(1924 Woman's Club Cook Book)

2 cups sugar
¼ cup cold water

1 cup cocoa
2 cups boiling water

1. Mix sugar and cocoa. Add cold water to dissolve mix.
2. Add boiling water and boil for 6 minutes.
3. Put in glass jar and keep cold.

GUAVA SAUCE

(Mrs. Wm. F. Bigoney, Jr.)

1 quart guavas (approx.)   1 cup water
1 cup sugar

1. Wash and peel guavas. Cut in half and scoop out seeds.
2. Put guavas, sugar and water in sauce pan. Boil about 20 minutes.
3. Cool in refrigerator several hours. Can be stored in refrigerator.

NOTE: Delicious as sauce on ice cream, etc.

COCONUT MILK I

(U. of Fla. Agr. Ext. Service
Circular 163)

Grind coconut with fine blade of food chopper or put through blender. If chopper is used, after chopping add 2 cups water or coconut milk from shell. For each two cups of chopped coconut, add two tablespoons sugar. Place in quart jar and shake. Strain by pouring through muslin bag or cheesecloth. Squeeze bag to get out all milk.

COCONUT MILK II

Add boiling water or coconut shell milk to the chopped pulp. Stir well. Put through muslin bag or cheese cloth and squeeze.

NOTE: May be used over fresh fruit such as papaya, bananas; as a sauce over ice cream; used as flavoring in cakes, cookies.

TAMARIND SYRUP

(Broward County Home
Demonstration Agent)

2 cups shelled tamarinds   6 cups water
(pressed down in cup)   5⅓ cups sugar

1. Pour water over tamarinds. Soak overnight. Add sugar and boil for 15 minutes. Strain through sieve, rubbing as much pulp through as possible.
2. Put pulp in pan and bring to boiling point. Pour into hot sterile jars and seal.

NOTE: Can be used over pudding, salads, desserts and as base for Tamarind drink.

GUAVA SYRUP

(U. of Fla. Agr. Service
Circular 207)

Firm ripe acid guavas   Sugar

1. Wash fruit and remove blossom and stem ends and any scars on skin.
2. Run fruit through fruit press to remove seed. Measure and put in heavy saucepan.
3. Depending on acidity of fruit, add 2 or more cups of sugar to 4 cups of pulp.
4. Cook rapidly for about 15 minutes, stirring often.
5. Pour into hot clean jars. Seal and process in boiling water bath for 10 minutes.

NOTE: This sauce is excellent for puddings, whips, gelatine desserts, topping for ice cream and salads.

MANGO SAUCE

(U. of Fla. Agr. Ext. Service
Circular 161)

2 pints green mangos, peeled   1½ cups sugar (or ½ sugar
and sliced   and ½ corn syrup)
1 cup water

1. Steam or cook mangos in water until tender. Depending on acidity of fruit add sugar. Mix and cook 5 minutes more.

NOTE: May be served as an applesauce would be served, or used as dessert, in sherbert or ice cream.

LOQUAT SAUCE

(Broward County Home

Demonstration Agent)

1. Wash loquats. Remove stem and blossom end. Cut and remove seed. Run through food chopper using medium blade.
2. Add 1 cup water to 4 cups loquat pulp. Cook until tender, adding more water if necessary.
3. When tender add 1 cup sugar. Cook 5 minutes.
4. Pour into sterile jars and seal. Process immediately, 5 minutes in boiling water bath.

VANILLA SAUCE

(Mrs. W. B. Snyder, 1924
Woman's Club Cook Book)

½ cup butter
1 tablespoon corn starch

1 cup sugar
2 cups boiling water

1. Cream butter and sugar.
2. Place corn starch in sauce pan. Moisten with 1 tablespoon cold water. Pour two cups boiling water over corn starch. Cook until clear.
3. Stir hot mixture into butter-sugar mixture. Add vanilla. Mix well and serve.

HARD SAUCE

(Mrs. Alvarez Stanford)

½ cup butter
1 cup sugar

Flavoring to taste (½ teaspoon
vanilla, rum, almond extract, etc.)

1. Cream butter in bowl and blend in sugar.
2. Add flavoring by the drop, mixing well and being sure to not let the sauce get runny.

NOTE: To be served over puddings, fruits, etc. See Berry Pudding for a use also.

GOLDEN SAUCE

(Mrs. A. D. Marshall, 1917 So.
Methodist Cook Book)

⅓ cup butter
3 eggs

1 cup sugar
3 tablespoons lemon juice

1. Cream butter and sugar. Separate eggs. Add yolks to butter mix and stir well. Add lemon juice.
2. Beat egg whites until stiff. Fold into butter mixture.
3. Put mixing bowl in pan of hot water. Stir for 5 minutes. Serve at once.

NEW RIVER & OLD COURTHOUSE, FORT LAUDERDALE, FLORIDA

Egg and Cheese Dishes

Hickety, pickety, my black hen,
She lays eggs for gentlemen; . . . .

Hickety Pickety
Nursery Rhyme
Anonymous

CHEESE FONDUE

(Mrs. George H. Kittredge, Jr.)

1 pound sliced cheese
3 eggs
1 teaspoon salt
Dash pepper

16 slices bread
1½ cups milk
Dash Worcestershire
Butter

1. Make 8 thick cheese sandwiches, removing crusts on bread.
2. Beat 3 eggs, add milk, salt, pepper, Worcestershire.
3. Butter baking dish. Lay cheese sandwiches in dish. Pour milk mixture over sandwiches.
4. Bake for 45 minutes at 350°.

WELSH RAREBIT

(Mrs. Spencer S. Thomas)

1 teaspoon mustard
½ pound cheese (New York State or equal)
1 tablespoon butter

1 teaspoon salt
2 eggs
1 cup milk

1. Separate eggs. Mix yolks, cheese, butter, salt and milk in saucepan. Cook until blended.
2. Beat egg whites. Cool yolk mixture and fold in egg whites.

NOTE: To serve, pour over toast, top with cooked bacon strips and place under broiler to heat. Add sprig parsley and sliced tomatoes for pretty plate.

OLD TIME RAREBIT (serves 4)

(Mrs. Tom G. Lively)

8 slices bread
½ cup red wine

½ pound sharp cheese, sliced
Optional: bacon crumbs

1. Toast bread until very dry and brown. Put on cookie sheet.
2. Pour wine over bread until wine soaked up.
3. Lay cheese in thick layer over bread.
4. Bake in oven for about 20 minutes at 350° (or until cheese has melted and is slightly brown).
5. Serve at once. Well-done bacon crumbs may be sprinkled over top.

CHEESE SOUFFLE (serves 8)

(Mrs. Warren Craven)

½ pound sharp cheese, cut up   Loaf of bread
½ pound butter   1 pint milk
 4 eggs, beaten   Dash salt

1. Measure loaf of bread to 8 inches long. Use this 8 inch section. Remove crusts and cut into tiny pieces.
2. Melt butter in pan. Add milk and eggs, dash of salt.
3. In lightly buttered casserole put layer of bread pieces, add layer of cheese, layer of bread and so on until all bread and cheese is used up.
4. Pour milk mixture on bread and cheese. Let stand at room temperature for 3 hours.
5. Place casserole in pan of water. Bake 1½ hours at 325°.

NOTE: May be served with several sauces such as mushroom soup, shrimp soup, creamed chicken.

GNOCCHI A LA ROMAINE (serves 6)

(Mrs. Charles Schwarm)

1 quart milk   1 stick butter
1 cup hominy grits (not the fast   1 teaspoon salt
  cooking kind)   ½ teaspoon pepper
1 cup grated Gruyere cheese   ⅓ cup Parmesan cheese, grated

1. Bring milk to boil in large saucepan. Cut butter into pieces and add to milk.
2. When butter melted add hominy grits, stirring constantly and bring to boil.
3. Cook until looks like cooked farina, remove from heat and add salt, pepper.
4. Beat hard for 5 minutes (or until creamy). Pour into flat casserole (13x9x2 inch) and let set.
5. Cut into rectangular pieces and overlap like fallen dominoes in smaller buttered casserole.
6. Sprinkle both cheeses over this.
7. To serve, heat for 30 minutes in 400° oven then slip under broiler long enough to lightly brown.

NOTE: May be made up ahead of time, even the day before and final cooking (step 7) just before serving.

CHEESE CUSTARD

(Mrs. Wm. G. Hardy)

3 eggs
1 cup coarsely grated Cheddar cheese

1 cup milk
⅛ teaspoon pepper

1. Beat eggs slightly. Add milk, cheese and pepper.
2. Pour into glass pie pan. Bake about 30 minutes at 350° or until set.

NOTE: May be served with meat or fish course.

MANICOTTI

(Mrs. Jay Forbes)

8 eggs
1 cup water
1½ pounds ricotta cheese
¼ cup chopped parsley
3 cups canned marinara sauce

2 teaspoons salt
1½ cups flour
½ cup grated Romano cheese
Dash pepper

1. Beat 6 eggs until light. Add ½ teaspoon salt, flour and beat until smooth.
2. On hot greased griddle, pour ladle of mixture and smooth out to about 5 inches in diameter. Cook over low heat until done all the way through. Do not brown. Do not turn over.
3. Lay pancake on paper towel and proceed to cook all batter until batter used up.
4. Combine cheese, parsley, 2 beaten eggs, 1½ teaspoons salt and pepper.
5. Spoon cheese mixture onto pancakes and fold pancakes into thirds, overlap folds.
6. Arrange on shallow baking pan. Pour marinara sauce over all.
7. Bake for 20 minutes at 375°.

NOTE: Serve with green salad, garlic bread and coffee.

MUSHROOM SOUFFLE

(Mrs. L. Coleman Judd)

2 cups milk
2 tablespoons butter
1½ cups mushrooms, cut fine
Dash Worcestershire
2 cups fine bread crumbs

½ cup grated cheese
3 eggs
1 teaspoon lime juice (or lemon)

1. Heat milk. Add bread crumbs, butter, cheese. Simmer 10 minutes. Cool.

2. Separate eggs. Add yolks to mixture, add Worcestershire and lime (or lemon) juice.

3. Beat egg whites stiff. Add to mixture. Pour into greased baking dish.

4. Bake at 350 until lightly brown (about 30 minutes).

BAKED EGGS

(Miss Beulah Bondi,
Pachira Garden Club)

6 hard cooked eggs
1½ tablespoons flour
¼ teaspoon salt
1 pint sour cream

Parmesan cheese, grated
2 tablespoons butter
¾ cup milk
Nutmeg

1. Slice eggs in half lengthwise. Place in greased casserole.

2. Make white sauce: Blend butter and flour in pan. Add salt and milk. Cook for 5 minutes or until thick. Remove from heat and add sour cream.

3. Pour white sauce mixture over eggs. Sprinkle top generously with nutmeg. Then sprinkle top with Parmesan cheese.

4. Place under broiler until heated but do not brown cheese.

EGG CROQUETTES

(Mrs. Robert S. Pendleton)

6 boiled eggs
4 tablespoons butter
½ teaspoon salt
¼ teaspoon pepper
1 teaspoon minced parsley

4 tablespoons flour
1 egg, beaten
Bread crumbs
1 cup milk

1. Peel boiled eggs. Put through chopper or mince fine.
2. Add salt, pepper and parsley.
3. Make thick white sauce: Melt butter, add flour and slowly pour milk into mixture. Stir and cook until thick.
4. Add egg mixture to white sauce. Mix. Put on plate and place in refrigerator for several hours to chill.
5. When chilled, form into small balls. Roll in beaten egg, then in bread crumbs.
6. Melt shortening in fry pan, at least 2 inches deep. Brown on all sides. (About 2 minutes each side.) Drain on paper towel and serve at once.

NOTE: 1 cup ground ham may be added to above plus ½ cup more milk to sauce.

EGGS BENEDICT (serves 4)

(Recipe Selection Committee)

8 eggs
8 slices ham

4 English muffins
Hollandaise sauce

1. Fry ham slices until browned.
2. Split muffins and toast.
3. Poach eggs in boiling salted water.
4. Put toasted muffin on plate, add ham slice, add poached egg and top with hollandaise. Serve at once.

CREOLE OMELETTE (serves 6)

(Mrs. T. F. Moore, 1917 So. Methodist Cook Book)

6 large tomatoes, skinned	1 chopped onion
1 chopped green pepper	2 tablespoons butter
1 tablespoon bread crumbs	Dash salt
6 eggs	Dash cayenne

1. Put 1 tablespoon butter in frying pan. Add bread crumbs and fry until brown. Add tomatoes, pepper, onion, salt and cayenne. Stew for about 45 minutes or until vegetables are tender.

2. Separate eggs. Beat yolks. Beat whites. Fold whites into yolks.

3. Put 1 tablespoon of butter in frying pan. Pour egg mixture in. Cook until set. Pour tomato mixture over eggs. Fold eggs in half over tomato mixture. Cook two more minutes. Serve at once.

CORN SOUFFLE

(Mrs. Wm. G. Hardy)

1 can corn	1 cup milk
2 eggs	1 tablespoon butter
1¼ teaspoons salt	2 tablespoons flour
Dash pepper	

1. Melt butter. Add flour and milk. Bring to boiling point. Add corn, salt, pepper.

2. Separate eggs. Beat yolks until thick and add to milk mixture. Beat egg whites until stiff. Fold into milk mixture.

3. Pour into buttered baking dish.

4. Bake for 25-30 minutes at 350°.

5. Serve at once.

THE RIVERSIDE HOTEL, FORT LAUDERDALE, FLORIDA

Hors D' Oeuvres

*Tell me what you eat, and I will tell
you what you are.*

Physiologie de Gout
Anthelme Brittat-Savarin
(1755-1826)

CRABMEAT HORS D' OEUVRES

(Mrs. John W. DeGroot)

2 teaspoons dry mustard
½ teaspoon pepper
2 tablespoons Worcestershire
2 raw eggs
1 pound cooked crab meat
Nut meats ground very fine

½ teaspoon salt
3 dashes Tabasco
1 tablespoon capers
4 tablespoons mayonnaise
6 large Sea Toast crackers
Butter

1. Crush the Sea Toast to make fine crumbs. Put in large bowl. Add mustard, salt, pepper, Tabasco, Worcestershire, capers, mayonnaise and raw eggs. Mix well.
2. Check crab for shell bits. Put crab in crumb mix. Mash well with fork. Spread on large flat platter and chill 2-3 hours.
3. When ready to use, roll into tiny balls. Roll balls in fine ground nuts.
4. Heat butter to cover bottom of fry pan. Brown crab balls.
5. Put each on toothpick and arrange on serving plate.

LOBSTER TAIL HORS D' OEUVRES

(Recipe Selection Committee)

4 boiled lobster tails
Hot hollandaise sauce

Package sliced bacon
Toothpicks and skewers

1. Remove lobsters from shell. Cut into about 1½ inch pieces.
2. Wrap each piece of lobster with slice of bacon. Thread about 5 wrapped pieces on each skewer. (If bacon has a tendency to slip, tack it with toothpick.)
3. Lay skewers on broiler rack about 3 inches from flame and brown (about 5 minutes), turn and brown on other side.
4. Place skewer on plate and pour hot hollandaise over each.
5. Can be left on skewers or removed and placed on individual toothpicks.

CONCH FRITTERS

(Mrs. Norman E. W. Oliver)

8 fresh conchs
2 tablespoons milk
1 teaspoon salt
1 teaspoon pepper
1 teaspoon baking powder

2 tablespoons lime juice
2 eggs
1 cup flour
Melted bacon fat and butter

1. Clean conchs. Put through meat grinder. Put lime juice on ground conch and mix.
2. In mixing bowl mix the flour, baking powder, salt and pepper. Add milk and eggs and mix.
3. Add conch mixture to flour mixture. Mix thoroughly.
4. In fry pan put enough bacon fat and butter (mixed half and half) to make about 1 inch of fat on bottom of pan. Heat smoking hot.
5. Drop conch mixture by teaspoonful into hot fat and fry until brown.

NOTE: Can be frozen. To use just drop onto hot pan, no additional fat necessary and heat until hot.

CURRIED SHRIMP DIAMONDS

(Mrs. P. Silvano)

⅔ cup soft butter
½ teaspoon salt
1 teaspoon water
1 cup finely chopped cooked shrimp

1½ cups sifted flour
1 teaspoon instant minced onion
1 teaspoon Worcestershire
1 teaspoon curry powder

1. Cut butter into flour and salt.
2. Soak instant onion in water and Worcestershire a few minutes.
3. Add shrimp, curry powder to flour mixture, stirring with fork until blended. Add onion. Mix well.
4. Roll out on floured board to ½ inch thick. Cut into diamond shapes. Put on greased cookie sheet.
5. Bake about 30 minutes at 375°. Can be served hot or cold.

NOTE: These diamonds can be frozen for later use.

SEA FOOD SPREAD

(Mrs. Nelson B. Thomas)

1 cup chopped shrimp
1 cup finely chopped lobster
½ cup chopped pistachio nuts

1 cup chopped crab meat
¾ cup Russian dressing

1. Mix sea foods and dressing. Refrigerate for at least one hour.
2. When ready to serve, sprinkle nuts on top of each one. To be served on thin crackers or melba toast.

CONCH SALAD CANAPE

(Mrs. Wm. F. Bigoney, Jr.)

4 cleaned raw conchs, chopped
   into small pieces
Juice of 2 small Key limes

2 tablespoons vinegar
1 small onion, chopped
½ green pepper, chopped

1. Mix chopped conch, onion, green pepper, lime juice, vinegar and chill at least one hour.
2. Serve on saltines or other soda type cracker.

PLANTAIN CHIPS (MARQUITAS)

(Recipe Selection Committee)

1 firm plantain

Cooking fat

1. Peel plantain. Cut diagonally in very thin slices.
2. Have fat hot in deep fry pan. Drop in slices. Fry as you would French fried potatoes.
3. When brown, remove from pan and drain on paper towelling. Sprinkle with salt and pepper.

HORS D' OEUVRES SUGGESTIONS

(Mrs. P. Silvano)

1. On bread cut-outs: Spread with butter, three tablespoons cavair, 3 tablespoons chopped onion. Garnish with mashed egg yolk.

2. Mix cream cheese and chopped stuffed olives. Spread on bread cut-outs.

3. Mix deviled ham, chopped hard cooked egg and horseradish. Use as spread.

4. Make spread of minced shrimp, chopped cucumber, minced onion and mayonnaise.

5. Make spread of ground chicken, chopped salted almonds and flaked coconut. Mix with mayonnaise.

6. Make spread of softened cream cheese, Roquefort. Beat until smooth with a little cream. Add chopped pecans.

7. To make shrimp butter: Put shrimp through blender, add butter and season with onion salt.

8. On cracker place slice hard salami, add small gherkin cut fan shape, decorate top with butter rose.

9. On cracker, place asparagus tip, red pickled tongue and decorate with butter.

10. Use Cheese Trees as finger snack. Recipe follows.

Cheese Trees:

¼ cup soft butter	Paprika
¼ teaspoon chili powder	¼ teaspoon salt
1 cup biscuit mix	1 cup grated sharp Cheddar cheese
Water	

1. Cut butter into biscuit mix. Add salt and chili powder. Add cheese. Add just enough water to hold mixture together.

2. Force dough through cookie gun with disc that forms trees. Put on cookie sheet. Sprinkle with paprika.

3. Bake for 10 minutes in 425° oven.

NOTE: These can be served hot or cold. They may be frozen

CHICKEN HORS D' OEUVRES SANDWICHES

(Miss Nola G. Bates)

3 cups water
1 small onion, chopped
½ teaspoon salt

1 cut up stewing chicken
2 chopped ribs of celery
Butter
Mayonnaise

1. Put water, onion, celery in stewing pan. Bring to boil. Add chicken slowly so water won't stop boiling. Cover pot, reduce heat and cook for 1 hour. Add salt. Cook for 1 more hour (or until chicken is tender). Remove chicken from broth. Bone chicken and place meat in refrigerator.
2. Strain broth. Put in refrigerator. Chill. When cold, remove fat from broth.
3. Chop chicken meat. Add enough broth to moisten meat.
4. Spread crackers, wafers or bread with butter. Spread layer of mayonnaise. Spread chicken on top.

NOTE: Chicken does not fall off wafers nor does it taste dry. An excellent chicken spread!

HOT HAM PUFFS

(Mrs. P. Silvano)

1 can (4½ ounce) deviled ham
3 tablespoons mayonnaise
Bread cut-outs

1 egg white
1 teaspoon sharp mustard

1. Cut sliced bread into pretty shapes. Do not use crust.
2. Spread deviled ham on bread.
3. Beat egg white until stiff. Add mayonnaise and mustard.
4. Spoon over ham on bread.
5. Slip under broiler until just hot and lightly brown. Serve at once.

SNACKS

(Mrs. Arch Campbell)

1 box Cherrio cereal
1 package pretzel sticks
2 pounds mixed nuts
1 teaspoon garlic salt
1 teaspoon savory salt
1 box Kix cereal

1 box Ralston Bits cereal
¾ pound butter (3 sticks or
    1½ cups melted butter)
1 teaspoon celery salt
2 teaspoons Worcestershire
    sauce

1. Mix dry cereals and nuts.
2. Melt butter and mix in garlic salt, celery salt, savory salt and Worcestershire sauce.
3. Pour over dry cereal and mix well.
4. Spread mixture on cookie sheet and place in 250° oven for about one hour, stirring frequently.
5. Can be stored in glass jars.

PARMESAN STICKS

(Mrs. P. Silvano)

4 slices bread
½ cup cornflakes
Dash onion salt

½ cup butter
¼ cup grated Parmesan cheese

1. Toast bread. Trim off crusts. Cut each slice into 5 sticks.
2. Melt butter. Dip sticks quickly into butter and arrange on baking pan.
3. Combine cornflakes, cheese and onion salt. Sprinkle over sticks.
4. Bake at 350° for 5 to 10 minutes, or until brown.

NOTE: These can be frozen. To serve, thaw and serve cold or re-heat in oven.

LIME-AVOCADO DIP

(Mrs. Tom G. Lively)

1 large ripe avocado (peeled and mashed)
2 tablespoons minced onion
½ teaspoon chili powder
1 tablespoon olive oil
1 fresh tomato (peeled and pushed through sieve)

2 tablespoons grated cheese (Cheddar or Parmesan)
½ teaspoon oregano
2 tablespoons lime juice

1. Beat all ingredients together. Put in covered dish and chill for about 1 hour.
2. Serve as dip or spread thickly on crackers.

AVOCADO CREAM CHEESE SPREAD

(Mrs. P. Silvano)

1 avocado
1 teaspoon lemon juice

1 package (3 ounce) cream cheese
Dash of sherry

1. Peel avocado. In bowl mash cheese, mash avocado, add lemon juice, mix well. Add enough sherry to moisten for spreading.
2. Will make enough spread for about 2 dozen canapes.

GUACAMOLE

(Recipe Selection Committee)

1 peeled mashed avocado
1 tablespoon minced onion
½ teaspoon Worcestershire
1 tablespoon lime juice

½ teaspoon salt
Optional: 1 small peeled finely chopped tomato

1. Beat all ingredients together.
2. Can be used as a dip, spread, filling.

CELERY-MUSHROOM BITS

(Mrs. Mary Ann May Wood)

4-5 large stalks celery
4 tablespoons sour cream
Dash Worcestershire
½ cup peeled chopped fresh
  mushrooms

Dash Tabasco
Dash salt
Dash pepper

1. Wash and dry celery stalks. Cut into 1 inch pieces.
2. In bowl mix mushrooms, sour cream, salt, pepper, Tabasco and Worcestershire.
3. Pile mushroom mix into celery bits.

SMOKY CHEESE DIP

(Mrs. Wm. G. Crawford)

⅓ cup pineapple juice
6 ounces cream cheese
1 small garlic clove, mashed

¼ teaspoon Worcestershire
6 ounces smoky cheese

1. Mix pineapple juice, Worcestershire and cream cheese. Blend smoky cheese and garlic. (If using blender, use high speed for 30 seconds.)

BLU CHEESE DIP

(Recipe Selection Committee)

2 4 ounce packages blu cheese
3 6 ounce packages cream
  cheese

2 tablespoons chopped onion
¼ cup milk
Dash of Worcestershire

1. Let all ingredients warm up to room temperature.
2. Mix all ingredients together. If still too stiff for a dip, add a little more milk.
3. Serve at room temperature.

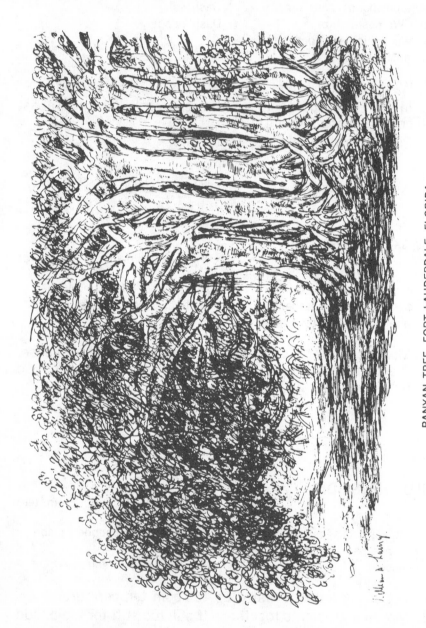

BANYAN TREE, FORT LAUDERDALE, FLORIDA

Jams, Jellies and Preserves

The fairest spot to me,
On the land or on the sea,
Is the charming little cupboard
Where the jam-pots grow.

Master Jack's Song
Laura Elizabeth Richards
(1850-1943)

KUMQUAT MARMALADE

(Mrs. Grover M. Davis)

2 quarts kumquats   3 limes or lemons
3 quarts water

1. Wash kumquats, cut in half and remove seeds. If you do not have a blender slice kumquats thin.
2. Slice limes thin, add to kumquats.
3. Put in enamel or stainless steel pot and cover with water. Let stand about 12 hours.
4. Boil mixture for about 20 minutes then let stand for 6 - 8 hours.
5. Fill blender ⅔ full of fruit and juice and coarsely chop. Repeat until all fruit is chopped.
6. Measure about 4-6 cups chopped fruit, adding 1 cup sugar for each cup fruit. If you have more fruit use more pans, putting maximum of 6 cups in each.
7. Boil sugar fruit mixture until thick enough to jell, about 30-40 minutes.
8. Put in sterile jars and seal.

~~~~~~~~~~~~~~~~~~~~~~~~

CALAMONDIN MARMALADE

(Mrs. Henry O. Patton)

About 4 cups ripe, firm fruit   Water
Sugar

1. Wash fruit. Remove blemishes. Cut in half and remove seeds. Put seeds in bowl and cover with water. Let stand overnight.
2. Chop peel and fruit. Measure chopped fruit. Put 1 cup water in pot for each cup chopped fruit. Let stand overnight.
3. Strain water from seeds. Save water.
4. Put watered chopped fruit on stove. Add water from seeds. Cook about 20 minutes or until fruit is tender.
5. In another pan, put 1 cup cooked fruit for each cup sugar. Bring to boil and cook until mixture jells (222°).
6. Pour into sterile jars and seal.

BANANA MARMALADE

(William Buck, Jr.)

1 cup ripe mashed banana   ½ cup sugar
1 teaspoon lime juice

1. Put mashed bananas, sugar, lime juice in pan. Bring to boil. Boil for 5 minutes.
2. Cool and put in jar. Keep in refrigerator.

Variations: For parties, add ¼ cup rum to banana marmalade and use as dunk, or spread. Mix 2 parts French dressing with 1 part banana marmalade for use on citrus or molded salads.

ORANGE MARMALADE

(Mrs. Frank Stranahan)

3 medium sized bright oranges   1 lemon
                                  9 cups water

1. Quarter oranges. Put through grinder using small or medium blade.
2. Juice the lemon and add to orange mix. Add rind of lemon whole. Add water.
3. Cook until tender (or until head of pin easily pierces a piece of orange peel). Remove from stove.
4. Cover pot and let stand until next day.
5. Measure one cup orange mix to one full cup sugar. Use no more than 3 cups of orange and 3 cups of sugar at one time.
6. Bring mix to boil. When mix begins to jell remove from fire at once. Pour into sterile jars and seal. (To check for jelling, put spoonful of orange mix on saucer on window sill. When it begins to wrinkle, it is jelling.)

NOTE: Do not overcook as mixture will toughen and darken.

APRICOT MANGO PRESERVES

(Mrs. Norman E. W. Oliver)

8 firm mangos
1 cup water

1 pound dried apricots
Sugar

1. In saucepan, put water and apricots and cook until apricots tender (approx. 15 minutes).
2. Peel and slice mangos. Add sliced mango to apricots, and cook together for about 15 minutes.
3. Measure 1 cup of cooked fruit and 1 cup of sugar and put in pan. Keep measuring cooked fruit and sugar in equal quantities and put in pan.
4. Boil mixture for about 10 minutes. Pour into sterilized jars and seal.

PAPAYA-GINGER-PINEAPPLE CONSERVE

(Recipe Selection Committee)

2 cups diced firm papaya
2 cups shredded or diced fresh
  pineapple
4 cups sugar

4 teaspoons grated fresh ginger
  root (or 4 teaspoons diced
  candied ginger)

1. Mix all ingredients in kettle. Bring to boil. Reduce heat and cook until thickens.
2. Pour into hot sterilized jars and seal.

NOTE: Use on ice cream, on toast, biscuits.

MANGO MARMALADE

(Mrs. W. P. Brobeck, 1924
Woman's Club Cook Book)

Ripe mangos   Sugar

1. Peel mangos. Push flesh through sieve.
2. For each cup of pulp, add 1 cup of sugar.
3. Cook until mixture thickens. Pour into sterile jars and seal.

KUMQUAT PRESERVES

(Mrs. Alfred J. Beck)

10 pounds kumquats   4 pounds sugar
1 rounded teaspoon soda

1. Wash fruit thoroughly. Trim blossom end and cut a slit ⅓ the length of each fruit.
2. In glass, stainless steel or enamel pan, put layer of fruit, layer of sugar until all used up. In center put soda. Do not stir. Do not add water. Let stand overnight.
3. To cook, place container over asbestos mat (or use simmer control). Using wooden or stainless steel spoon, gently lift fruit around in pot. Do not stir around.
4. When enough syrup has formed to prevent burning, increase heat so contents will boil. Reduce heat and simmer about 2 hours (or until kumquats are tender). Avoid burning.
5. Pour into sterilized jars and seal.

ROSELLE CONSERVE

(Broward County Home
Demonstration Agent)

5 cups roselle   1 cup seeded raisins
1 orange   3 cups sugar
1 cup broken pecan meats   Water

1. Grate rind from orange. Slice very thin. Discard seed and center pith. Add 1 cup water and simmer until tender.
2. Remove roselle pod by slicing both ends and press with fingers. Add 3¼ cups water and cook for 10 minutes. Add to cooked orange. Add raisins and sugar and cook quickly until mixture thickens. Add nuts, cook 5 minutes longer.
3. Pour into sterile jars, process 10 minutes, seal.

MANGO JAM

(Mrs. D. T. Hart,
1924 Woman's Club Cook Book)

3 pounds mangos, peeled
2 lemons, juice, rind
1 tablespoon cinnamon
1 pint water

3 pounds sugar
1 tablespoon grated white ginger
root (or candied ginger)

1. Push mango flesh through sieve. Stir in sugar, cinnamon, ginger, water, juice of 2 lemons and 3 tablespoons rind.
2. Bring mixture to boil and simmer until thick.
3. Pour into sterile jars and seal.

RIPE PAPAYA JAM

(U. of Fla. Agr. Ext. Service
Circular 162)

6 cups ripe papaya pulp
5 cups sugar

½ cup lemon juice (or lime juice
or calamondin)

1. Press ripe papaya through coarse sieve. Then measure. Boil briskly in heavy pan until thick enough for jam.
2. Add lemon juice and sugar and continue to boil until thick and clear. Stir often to prevent burning.
3. Pour into hot clean jars and seal.
4. Store in cool, dark place.

LOQUAT JAM

(Broward County Home
Demonstration Agent)

1 quart fresh loquats
1½ cups sugar

1 cup water
2 teaspoons lemon juice

1. Wash, scald, peel and seed the fruit. Put through food chopper.
2. Add sugar to water and bring to boil, making a syrup. Add chopped fruit and cook to jellying point (225½°).
3. If loquats are sweet, add lemon juice while cooking.
4. Pour into sterile jars and seal.

PINEAPPLE JAM

(Mrs. R. G. Snow, 1924 Woman's
Club Cook Book)

Pineapple   Sugar

1. Peel, grate or chop as many pineapples as are desired.
2. Weigh and allow 1 pound of sugar to 1 pound pineapple. Mix sugar and pineapple well. Put in cool place overnight.
3. In morning place pot on stove and cook for ½ hour, or until soft enough to push through sieve. Put through coarse sieve. Return to pot.
4. Continue cooking, stirring constantly for about ½ hour or until a clear amber stage is reached.
5. Put into sterile jars and seal.

BASIC TROPICAL JELLY

(Recipe Selection Committee)

1. In 2 - 3 quart saucepan, put ripe fruit to no more than halfway up sides. Add a handful of underripe fruit.
2. Cover fruit with water. Boil until fruit is soft and you can either strain, mash or sieve it.
3. Pour pulp into jelly bag and let drip, some can be squeezed and others will form a cloudy jelly if squeezed.
4. Measure equal amount of juice and sugar, but do not cook too much at one time. (If you start out with the ½ saucepan of fruit, you will have the right amount to cook at one time.)
5. Bring sugar-juice mixture to boil. Cook until jelly stage is reached.
6. Pour into sterile jars and seal.

NOTE: Above can be used for:
    Berry Jelly - can squeeze bag
    Loquat Jelly - can squeeze bag (if too sweet add lime juice)
    Surinam Cherry Jelly - bag can be squeezed
    Pitomba Jelly - bag can be squeezed
    Governor's Plum Jelly - bag can be squeezed

SEA GRAPE JELLY

(Mrs. Truman G. Lively)

As many cups ripe sea grapes as
will half fill saucepan

Sugar
Water

1. Pick about half a saucepan of ripe sea grapes. Toss in a handful of green or reddish grapes.
2. Just cover with water and bring to boil. Cook until soft. Mash.
3. Put pulp in jelly bag and let drip.
4. Measure equal juice and sugar but do not cook more than 3 cups juice at one time.
5. Cook equal parts juice and sugar until thickens and jells on spoon. Pour into sterile jars and seal.

~~~~~~~~~~~~~~~~~~~~~~~~

GUAVA JELLY

(Recipe Selection Committee)

4 cups guava juice   4 cups sugar

1. Put juice and sugar in saucepan. Stir. Bring to **rapid** boil. Reduce heat to just below boiling. Cook until it is ready to jell (or temperature reaches 222°).
2. Pour into sterile jars. Skim foam off each jar and seal.

~~~~~~~~~~~~~~~~~~~~~~~~

CARISSA PLUM JELLY

(Broward County Home
Demonstration Agent)

Carissa plums   Water
Sugar

1. Select carissa plums that are whole, ripe and firm.
2. Put in saucepan. Cover with water and cook until soft.
3. Strain through jelly bag, allowing juice to drip. Do not squeeze bag.
4. For each cup of juice, add 1 cup of sugar. Boil rapidly until jelly stage is reached.
5. Pour into sterile jars and seal.

ROSELLE JELLY

(Broward County Home
Demonstration Agent)

Roselle   Sugar
Water

1. Remove pod from roselle by cutting both ends and press-
   ing with fingers.
2. Put roselle in saucepan using 2 cups of water for each
   cup of roselle. Bring to boil and boil for 10 minutes (or
   10 degrees Centigrade). Do not overcook. Allow to cool.
3. Put roselle in jelly bag and allow to drip.
4. For each cup of roselle juice add ¾ cup sugar. Bring to
   boil and cook to jelly stage (222° F).
5. Pour into sterile jars and seal.

NEWBILL CRANBERRY JELLY

(Mrs. Thomas J. Newbill)

Package of cranberries   Sugar

1. Put cranberries in kettle and just cover with water. When
   tender, strain through food mill to get pulp without skins.
2. Use equal portions of pulp and sugar. Mix and bring to
   boil. Put in dash of salt.
3. Pour into serving dishes or glasses and allow to set.
   Refrigerate.

WINE JELLY

(Godey's Lady's Book, 1869)

1 box unflavored gelatin (or 3   3 sticks cinnamon
  envelopes)   2 lemons, juiced, rind of 1
2 cups cold water   6 cups boiling water
2 cups wine (Madeira, or orange   1¼ pounds sugar
  juice)

1. Put gelatin in cold water. Add cinnamon, juice of lemons,
   rind, and let stand for 1 hour. Add boiling water, wine
   and sugar. Bring to boil. Remove from fire and strain
   though jelly bag or cloth.
2. Pour wine jelly into flat dish and put in refrigerator.
3. Next day use sharp knife and cut into half-inch squares.
   Can be stored in refrigerator in covered dishes.

NOTE: This is not a dessert. To be served with meat or fowl course.

101

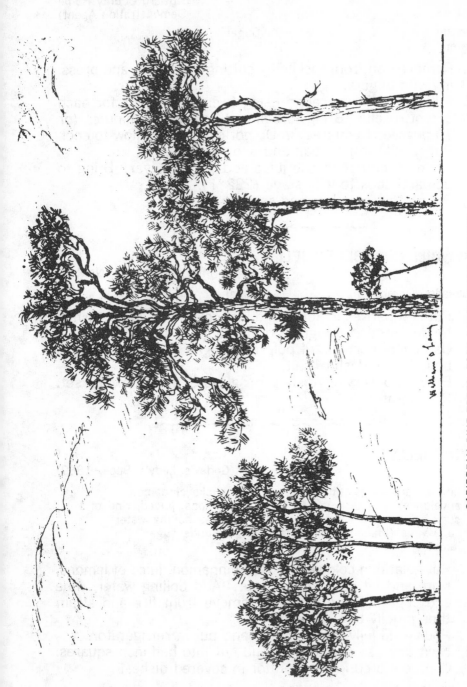

CARIBBEAN PINE TREES, FORT LAUDERDALE, FLORIDA

Meat

And make me savory meat such as I love, and
bring it to me, that I may eat; . . . .

Holy Bible
Genesis 27:4

BEEF STROGANOFF SUPREME (serves 10)

(Mrs. James D. Camp, Jr.)

1 cup butter	1½ cups finely chopped onion
1½ pounds fresh mushrooms	3½ pounds beef (top round) cut
6 tablespoons flour	into strips ¼x¼x2 inches
3 cups bouillon	1½ teaspoons salt
6 tablespoons tomato paste	2 teaspoons Worcestershire
¾ cup sour cream	1½ cups heavy cream
	8 cups fluffy rice

1. Melt ⅓ cup butter in large pan. Add onions and saute until golden. Remove onions. Melt ⅓ cup more butter. Add sliced mushrooms and saute until lightly brown. Remove mushrooms. Melt remaining butter in pan.
2. Dredge beef in flour. Saute in butter until brown.
3. Add bouillon, salt, onions. Cover and simmer until beef is tender (about 1½ hours).
4. Stir in tomato paste, Worcestershire sauce, sour cream, heavy cream and mushrooms. Heat thoroughly. Serve over rice.

KING-SIZE STEAK BITS

(Mrs. George H. Gore)

1 steak, sirloin about 3¾ pound cut 2 inches thick	1 clove garlic
1 tablespoon dry mustard	½ cup melted butter
1 cup red wine	½ teaspoon Worcestershire
Dash pepper	Dash Tabasco

1. Mix wine, crush garlic and put in wine. Marinate steak for at least 2 hours, more is better.
2. Mix melted butter, mustard, salt, pepper, Worcestershire and Tabasco, heat mixture.
3. Drain steak. Broil about 3 inches from flame for 15 minutes or until done to personal taste. Cut into king-sized pieces.
4. Place cut up steak bits in chafing dish. Pour butter sauce over steak.

NOTE: Can be used as main dish or on toothpicks as canapes.

BRITTANY BEEF (serves 6)

(Mrs. Dudley R. Stokes)

3 pounds stew meat cut into cubes
¼ cup flour
½ teaspoon pepper
1 teaspoon dried parsley or several sprigs fresh
1 carrot, sliced

1½ cups red wine
1 cup consomme
½ teaspoon salt
½ teaspoon thyme
12 small white onions
1½ cups fresh mushrooms
Butter

1. Mix flour, salt, pepper, thyme. Dredge meat. Melt enough butter to cover bottom of Dutch oven and brown meat.
2. Add wine, consomme, parsley, onions and slowly simmer for about 2 hours or until meat tender.
3. Discard pieces of carrot. Add mushrooms and heat for 5 more minutes.

NOTE: Can be prepared the day before. Just heat to serve. Will make complete meal along with salad, bread and coffee.

HAMBURGER PIE (serves 6)

(Mrs. Ralph R. Lehr)

½ pound ground beef (round steak)
¾ cup chopped celery
1 can tomato sauce (8 ounce)
1 teaspoon Worcestershire
1 tablespoon chopped parsley
½ recipe of Stir-n-Roll Biscuit dough

1 tablespoon oil
1 onion chopped
¼ cup chopped green pepper
½ teaspoon salt
Dash pepper
½ teaspoon celery seed

1. Heat oil in fry pan. Add meat and brown. Add onion, celery, green pepper. Cook for 5 minutes. Stir in tomato sauce, Worcestershire, salt and pepper.
2. Put mixture into deep pie pan or oven pan (or 8 inch round deep pan).
3. Make Stir-n-Roll dough. Add parsley and celery seed to dough. Roll to fit pan. Place over hot meat.
4. Bake 15 minutes at 450°. Remove from oven and let stand for 5 minutes.
5. Serve from dish or invert over platter and serve.

NOTE: See Index for Stir-n-Roll Biscuits.

SKEWERED FLANK STEAK (serves 4)

(Mrs. Richard A. LaPointe)

1 medium flank steak	½ cup oil
¼ cup vinegar	1 tablespoon capers
½ cup chopped onion	1 bay leaf
1 teaspoon salt	⅛ teaspoon pepper
¼ cup shredded sharp cheese	2 tablespoons parsley
2 cans corn (12 ounce)	3 tomatoes

1. Combine oil, vinegar, capers, onion, bay leaf, salt, pepper, in saucepan. Cook over low flame 5 minutes.
2. Place steak in shallow pan. Pour hot oil over. Cover and place in refrigerator at least 6 hours. Turn occasionally.
3. Remove meat from marinade. Place on board. Sprinkle with cheese and parsley. Start with long side and roll steak. Cut into 1½ inch pieces and skewer each.
4. Arrange corn in bottom of broiler pan. Put rack over corn. Arrange meat pinwheels on rack.
5. Place in preheated broiler 3 inches from flame for 10 minutes. Turn meat. Broil 5 minutes longer.
6. Slice tomatoes in half. Place on rack with meat. Brush with butter, broil 5 minutes. Serve at once.

BEEF STROGANOFF (serves 6)

(Mrs. John E. Morris)

1½ pounds round steak cut into thin strips	Flour, salt, pepper
	¼ cup butter
1 can drained mushrooms (4 ounce)	½ cup diced onions
	1 can beef bouillon
1 garlic clove, chopped	Cooked noodles or rice
1 cup sour cream	

1. Dredge strips of meat in seasoned flour.
2. Melt butter in pan, brown meat and onions. Add mushrooms, garlic and beef bouillon.
3. Cover and cook 1 hour or until meat is tender, stirring occasionally.
4. Slowly stir in sour cream and cook for 5 more minutes.
5. Serve over hot noodles (about 3 cups) or hot rice.

MOUSSAKA

(Mrs. Henry O. Patton)

1 pound chopped beef
1 chopped onion
Dash salt
Dash pepper
Dash nutmeg
3 ounces bread crumbs

1 tablespoon chopped parsley
½ stick butter (⅛ pound)
1 small can tomato sauce
2 small eggplants (or 1 large)
1 cup grated cheese
½ cup white wine

White Sauce:
1 pint milk
1 cup flour
2 tablespoons butter
1 egg

Dash salt
Dash pepper
Dash nutmeg

1. Brown onions in butter. Add chopped meat, mix until crumbly. Add tomato sauce, wine, salt, pepper, parsley and nutmeg. Cover and simmer for one hour.
2. Cut egg plant into pieces about ¼ inch thick. Fry in deep fat until brown.
3. Make white sauce: Melt butter, mix flour, egg, salt, pepper and milk. Cook until very thick.
4. In shallow greased pan, arrange fried eggplant. Sprinkle with few bread crumbs.
5. Remove meat from heat, add ½ cup grated cheese and rest of bread crumbs. Spread over eggplant. Pour white sauce over eggplant. Sprinkle rest of cheese on top.
6. Bake for 15 minutes at 375° or until top golden brown.
7. Cool slightly and cut into squares to serve.

CHILI CON CARNE (serves 8)

(Mrs. Wm. G. Crawford)

3 tablespoons salad oil
1 cup chopped onions
2 pounds ground beef
2 cans tomatoes (19 ounce each)
2 teaspoons chili powder

¼ cup chopped green pepper
1 clove garlic chopped
2 cans kidney beans (17 ounce each)
1½ teaspoons salt
⅓ cup water

1. Heat oil in large skillet. Add green pepper, onions, garlic and beef. Saute until brown. Stir often. Add beans, tomatoes, salt and chili powder. Mix well.
2. Simmer mixture about ½ hour. Stir often. If mixture becomes too thick, add a little water.

NOTE: Has better flavor if made day before using. Heat to serve. Two cups chopped ham may be added for additional flavor.

BRAISED BEEF TONGUE

(Mrs. Charles L. Pierce)

1 fresh or brine cured tongue (about 4 pounds)
Flour
Dash salt
Dash pepper
1 cup chopped celery
½ cup chopped onion
2 cups canned tomatoes
1 bay leaf
6 whole cloves
Cooking oil
½ cup chopped parsley
1 cup chopped carrot
1 can mushrooms

1. Cook tongue about 2 hours in salted water with bay leaf and cloves. When tender, remove from water and peel.
2. Roll tongue in flour which has dash salt and pepper. Brown in skillet or Dutch oven in oil.
3. Add celery, parsley, onion, carrots, tomatoes. Cook until tender.
4. Just before serving, add mushrooms. Serve on platter placing vegetables on top.

~~~~~~~~~~~~~~~~~~~

BEEF NOODLEBAKE

(Mrs. Mitchell M. Benton)

2 tablespoons butter
1 pound ground round steak
1 tablespoon sugar
1 clove garlic
1 package (3 ounce) cream cheese
½ cup grated Cheddar cheese
2 cans tomato sauce
1 package (8 ounce) of noodles (medium sized)
6 small scallions
1 cup sour cream
Dash salt
Dash pepper

1. Melt butter in skillet. Fry beef until brown.
2. Crush garlic, add to meat. Add salt, pepper, sugar and tomato sauce. Cook slowly about 30 minutes.
3. Cook noodles and drain.
4. Chop scallions (include some of top parts) and mix with cream cheese and sour cream. Add dash salt and pepper.
5. In 2 quart casserole, put about ⅓ of noodles, add about ⅓ of cream cheese mix, add about ⅓ of meat mix. Repeat layers until finished. Sprinkle with Cheddar cheese.
6. Bake in 350° oven for about 40 minutes or until bubbly.

NOTE: Can be made a day ahead of time

CURRY AND PILAU

(Rev. Wm. E. Brooks)

Curry:

2 medium onions diced
4 fresh tomatoes diced
4 medium potatoes diced
1 teaspoon cinnamon
Dash salt

1 chicken
¼ teaspoon red pepper
1 tablespoon curry
Dash ginger

Pilau:

1 pound cubed beef
2 medium onions, chopped
　　fine
1½ cups rice

1 tablespoon curry
1 tablespoon cinnamon
1 tablespoon ginger
Sprinkle of red pepper

Curry:

1. Place cut up chicken in saucepan with water to cover. Cook until tender. Bone chicken. Add onions, tomatoes, potatoes and seasonings to broth. Add chicken meat to broth. Cook until potatoes are tender.

Pilau:

1. Brown cubed beef in oil in saucepan. Cover beef with water. Tie spices in spice bag and drop into beef water mixture. Boil gently until beef is tender. Drain broth from beef and save. Throw away spice bag.
2. In another pan use enough oil to brown chopped onions and raw rice. Add broth from beef. Cook until rice is done. Add beef.
3. Serve Pilau on plate and cover it with Curry.

ONE DISH DINNER (serves 4)

(Mrs. Curtis D. Benton, Jr.)

1 pound ground beef
1 can white shoe peg corn

1 medium onion, chopped
1 can tomatoes.

1. Brown beef and onions in little oil.
2. In baking dish, put layer of meat, layer of corn, then layer of tomatoes.
3. Bake for 1 hour at 350°.

SWEDISH MEAT BALLS

(Mrs. C. W. Schlueter)

1 pound ground beef
½ cup chopped onion
1 egg
1 egg white
Dash salt
Dash pepper
2 cups bouillon

½ pound ground pork (or pork sausage)
½ cup raw grated potato
1 cup milk
Butter
1 tablespoon flour

1. Put potato in milk and soak.
2. Put enough butter in bottom of fry pan to cover and brown onions in butter.
3. Mix beef, pork, onion, egg and egg white, potato, salt and pepper. Put in refrigerator to harden (about 2 hours). Make into small balls about size of walnut.
4. Fry meat balls in oil until browned. Discard oil.
5. In butter in which onions were fried, add flour. Add the boullion. Bring to boil and simmer 5 minutes.
6. Put meat balls in baking dish. Strain bouillon over meat balls.
7. Bake 1 hour at 350°.

NOTE: Can be used as main dish or on toothpicks as canapes.

ENGLISH BEEFSTEAK AND KIDNEY PIE

(Mrs. J. Lionel Lazonby)

1 pound best cut of beefsteak
Flour
Salt
Pepper

Water
½ pound kidneys
Pastry mix for pies

1. Cut beef and kidney into 1 inch cubes. Dredge in flour which has been seasoned with salt and pepper.
2. Put into pan and just barely cover with water. Simmer for about 2 hours with lid on pan. Do not allow mixture to dry.
3. Make light, flaky pastry and line individual pie dishes with pastry about 2 inches deep. Pour meat mixture into dishes and put crust on top.
4. Bake for about 20 minutes at 375° or until top crust is brown.

NOTE: Decorate top crust with two leaves of pastry covered with pastry rose (to make rose, pinch together two squares of pastry).
To increase recipe: Use two parts beefsteak to one part kidneys.
To hold up top crust: Invert small egg cup in meat mixture before putting top crust on and rest crust against cup.

MEAT LOAF

(Arch Campbell)

2 pounds ground chuck roast
½ medium green pepper
1 medium onion
6 slices bread
2 eggs
⅛ teaspoon white pepper
½ teaspoon Worcestershire

⅛ pound ground pork sausage
3 small stalks celery
½ cup fresh or 2 tablespoons dried parsley
½ cup milk
½ teaspoon seasoned salt
½ teaspoon Accent

1. Grate pepper, celery and onions on medium grater.
2. Slightly beat eggs and add milk.
3. Add pepper, Worcestershire, parsley, salt, Accent and break bread into small pieces into mix. Stir thoroughly.
4. Add meat to mixture. Do not handle more than necessary as over-handling will toughen.
5. Shape into loaf and place in greased oblong baking dish (not loaf pan).
6. Bake for 1½ hours at 350°.
7. If gravy desired, drain off grease and use both broth and brownings.

MEAT BALLS IN SOUR CREAM (serves 6)

(Recipe Selection Committee)

1 pound ground beef
1 egg
1 tablespoon minced onion
Dash salt
Dash pepper
3 tablespoons flour
1 cup sour cream

1 cup soft bread crumbs
¼ cup milk
1 clove garlic, crushed
3 tablespoons butter
1 can tomatoes (19 ounce)

1. Mix meat, crumbs, egg, onion, garlic salt, pepper, milk. Form into 18 small balls.
2. Melt butter in fry pan. Brown balls. Remove from pan. Add flour to pan, add tomatoes, stir. Add meat balls. Cook for 20 minutes. Add sour cream. Heat for 5 more minutes.
3. Serve at once.

ITALIAN MEAT LOAF

(Mrs. Vincent Coppola, Sr.
Pachira Garden Club)

1½ pounds ground beef
½ pound ground pork
¼ cup warm water
Dash chopped parsley
Dash salt
Dash pepper
Tomato sauce (or spaghetti sauce)

4 slices bread with crusts removed
½ cup grated Parmesan cheese
2 eggs
1 clove garlic, chopped fine

1. Break bread into crumbs and put to soak in warm water.
2. Mix beef, pork, cheese, parsley and bread crumbs. Add eggs, salt, pepper and garlic. Mix well with hands.
3. Put into square pan and bake for ½ hour at 350°.
4. Cover with tomato sauce and bake for another ½ hour at 350°.
5. Serve with peas and mushrooms.

STUFFED MEAT LOAF

(Mrs. Vincent Coppola, Sr.
Pachira Garden Club)

Mix one Italian Meat Loaf
¼ cup butter
Dash salt
Dash pepper
2 tablespoons parsley
2 tablespoons water
2 tablespoons melted butter

½ cup chili sauce
3 medium onions, chopped
1½ cups soft bread crumbs
½ teaspoon sage
1 chopped green pepper
1 egg
½ cup water

1. Make Italian Meat Loaf, do not bake. Line bottom and sides of square pan with meat loaf mixture.
2. In ¼ cup butter, saute onions until transparent. Add bread crumbs, salt, pepper, sage, parsley, green pepper and 2 tablespoons water. Saute until golden brown. Remove from heat.
3. Slightly beat egg. Add to bread crumb mixture. Spread over meat loaf mixture in pan. Put remaining meat loaf mixture on top of crumb mixture.
4. Brush top of meat loaf with 2 tablespoons melted butter. Add water and chili sauce.
5. Bake for 45 minutes at 350°.

VEAL PROVOLONE (serves 6)

(Mrs. Curtis D. Benton, Jr.)

6 thin slices veal, pounded as for scallopine
½ pound fresh mushrooms (or 6 ounce can)

4 thin slices boiled ham
6 slices Provolone cheese
¼ cup chicken broth
½ cup white wine

1. Saute veal until browned. Place in shallow flat baking dish, one layer deep.
2. Frizzle ham slices (fry in hot butter quickly). Put ham on top of veal. Add layer of cheese.
3. Saute mushrooms if using fresh. Put mushrooms on top of cheese.
4. In pan used to cook meat, put broth and wine. Cook gently about 3 minutes. Pour over casserole.
5. Bake about 15 minutes at 375° or until heated through and cheese melted.

NOTE: This may be made early in the morning and baked at the last minute.

CREAMED DRIED BEEF ON TOAST

(Recipe Selection Committee)

¼ pound dried beef
2 tablespoons minced onion
1 cup milk
Salt and pepper to taste

¼ cup butter
3 tablespoons flour
1 cup sour cream
8 pieces of toast cut diagonally

1. Cut beef into bite sizes.
2. In saucepan melt butter. Add onion and cook for 5 minutes. Blend in flour. Gradually add milk and cook for 5 more minutes or until thick. Remove from heat. Add beef, sour cream. Re-heat but do not boil. Add salt and pepper.
3. Arrange toast (2 slices per serving) on plate. Spoon dried beef mixture over toast. Serve at once.

WIENER SCHNITZEL

(Mrs. Robert C. Bishop)

1 pound veal steak
2 tablespoons water
Butter
Lemon juice

2 eggs
Bread crumbs
Salt

1. Selection and the cutting of the meat is of the utmost importance. It must be top grade veal steak, preferably sirloin and cut ⅛ - ¼ inch and pounded. The smaller the steak, the easier to handle.
2. Pound steaks well. Dip in bread crumbs.
3. Beat eggs and water for batter. Dip breaded meat into egg batter then again into crumbs.
4. Melt butter and dash of lemon juice in pan. Fry meat until crusty and golden brown.
5. Garnish with parsley or watercress.

VEAL CHOPS WITH SHERRY (serves 4)

(Recipe Selection Committee)

4 veal chops
1 egg
1 tablespoon lime juice
¼ cup dry sherry

Flour with salt, pepper

Butter
½ cup water

1. Dip veal in seasoned flour, then into beaten egg and back into flour.
2. Melt butter in bottom of fry pan (enough to cover bottom well) and when hot put in veal. Brown on both sides.
3. Add lime juice to water and pour over veal. Cover and simmer until tender (about 2 hours). Check often and if dry, add more water.
4. When tender, add sherry. Cook for 5 more minutes.
5. Remove meat from liquid. Thicken with flour and cook 5 minutes.
6. Arrange veal on platter, pour gravy over and serve at once.

BAKED HAM WITH GINGER ALE

(Mrs. Arch Campbell)

1 baking ham, pre-cooked
Dry mustard
Vinegar

2 bottles ginger ale
Brown sugar
Cloves

1. Put ham in roaster. Add two bottles ginger ale. Bake at 325° for about 1 hour. Remove from oven.
2. Skin ham. Make a paste of dry mustard, brown sugar and a little vinegar. Spread on ham. Stick with cloves.
3. Bake for 30 minutes at 325° or until light brown.

ORANGE GLAZE PORK CHOPS (serves 4)

(Mrs. Richard E. Lewis)

4 pork chops cut at least 1 inch thick

2 oranges - 1 sliced and 1 for juice

Stuffing:

¼ cup diced onion
1 cup broken bread bits
2 tablespoons butter
¼ teaspoon allspice
Dash salt
Dash pepper

¼ cup diced celery
1 egg
¼ cup orange juice
¼ teaspoon rosemary

1. Melt butter in large frying pan. Add onion and celery and cook until onions become transparent.
2. In bowl mix eggs, orange juice, salt, pepper, rosemary, allspice. Add onions, celery and bread bits, mix well. The mixture should be sticky.

1st Glaze:
Mix ¼ cup honey and ¼ cup orange juice.
2nd Glaze:
Mix ¼ cup honey and 1 tablespoon orange juice.

1. Brown pork chops in pan in which onions and celery cooked.
2. Make slot in pork chops and stuff.
3. Arrange chops in shallow baking pan and put slice of orange on top of each one, pour 1st Glaze over chops, cover with lid or foil.
4. Bake for ½ hour at 350°. Remove lid.
5. Brush some of 2nd Glaze over chops and return uncovered to oven.
6. Bake uncovered for about 30 minutes more, brushing with remainder of 2nd Glaze every 10 minutes or until Glaze is gone.

SAUSAGE CASSEROLE A LA WESTCHESTER

(Mrs. Dwight L. Rogers, Jr.)

½ cup uncooked white
   unprocessed rice
1 pound sausage meat
1 package chicken noodle soup
   mix

1½ cups diced celery
1 medium onion, yellow
1 small green pepper
½ cup blanched and toasted
   almonds

1. Boil diced celery until tender. Drain.
2. Cook rice until about one-half done.
3. Fry sausage. Break into small bits and remove from fat.
4. In sausage fat, fry onions until clear. Drain and discard the fat.
5. Cook soup mix in 2½ cups water. Cook down until only about 2 cups remain. Add rice, sausage, celery, onion. Pour into casserole dish.
6. Add green pepper to top of mixture.
7. Bake for 30 minutes at 350°. Add almonds to top. Bake another 15 minutes.

BOILED PIG'S FEET

(Recipe Selection Committee)

1. Wash and clean feet. Place in pot, cover with water. Bring to rapid boil. Reduce heat and simmer for 4 - 6 hours or until tender. Salt may be added to water if you wish.

PICKLED PIG'S FEET

(Recipe Selection Committee)

1. Use recipe for boiled pig's feet. Drain.
2. In glass or enamel container put boiled pig's feet. Mix half vinegar and half water and pour over pig's feet, covering feet.
3. Refrigerate for 2 or 3 days before using.

HAM LOAF

(Miss Elizabeth Calerdine)

3 cups ground cooked ham	2 eggs
1 medium onion	1 cup milk
1 teaspoon dry mustard	1 teaspoon prepared mustard
½ chopped green pepper	½ cup catsup (or chili sauce)
1½ cups bread crumbs (or dry dressing crumbs)	

1. Grind ham, onion and pepper medium coarse.
2. Mix eggs, milk, mustard, catsup, well. Add crumbs.
3. Combine ham mix with egg mix. Shape into loaf. Put in shallow loaf pan.
4. Bake for 1 hour at 350°.

BARBECUED RIBS (serves 4)

(Recipe Selection Committee)

4-5 pounds ribs   2 cups Barbecue Sauce

1. Cut ribs into pieces for eating.
2. In large kettle put ribs, water to cover and ½ cup of Barbecue Sauce. Bring to boil, reduce heat and cook for 30 minutes. Drain.
3. Put ribs in shallow pan, pour 1 cup barbecue sauce over them and let marinate in sauce for about 8 hours, turning often.
4. Place ribs on rack. Brush with part of remaining sauce and broil for 20 minutes, brushing with sauce if they become dry. Turn and broil for 20 minutes on other side. Brush with sauce if become dry.

   or:

Place on baking pan. Pour over remaining sauce and bake for one hour at 350°. Brush with sauce every 15 minutes.

   or:

Place over white hot charcoal on rack. Turn every 10 minutes, basting often. Total cooking time will be 40 minutes.

MUSTARD SAUCE FOR HAM (1 pint)

(Mrs. Walter B. Hilliard,
Pachira Garden Club)

1 cup dry mustard (2 small cans) 2 eggs
1 cup Heinz vinegar 1 cup granulated sugar

1. Stir mustard and vinegar to a smooth paste and let soak overnight or half a day.
2. Add beaten eggs and sugar.
3. Cook in double boiler for one hour, stirring occasionally.

~~~~~~~~~~~~~~~~~~~~~~~~

RAISIN SAUCE

(Recipe Selection Committee)

1 box seedless raisins ½ cup vinegar
Enough water to cover ⅔ cup brown sugar

1. Soak raisins in water for 2 hours. Put on stove and boil until half the water is boiled out. Add vinegar and sugar. Boil, reduce heat and simmer for about 10 minutes.

NOTE: Delicious with baked ham or any other meat.

~~~~~~~~~~~~~~~~~~~~~~~~

BARBECUE SAUCE (3 cups)

(Mrs. Tom G. Lively)

2 tablespoons butter 1 medium chopped onion
1 clove garlic 3 stalks celery
1 No. 2 can tomatoes 1 small can tomato sauce
3 tablespoons brown sugar ¼ cup vinegar
2 teaspoons dry mustard ½ teaspoon allspice
½ teaspoon clove 1½ teaspoons salt
1 chopped green pepper

1. In saucepan melt butter. Saute onion, mashed garlic and celery. Do not brown.
2. Add tomatoes, tomato sauce, sugar, vinegar, mustard, allspice, ground clove, salt and green pepper.
3. Simmer for about ½ hour. Stir to prevent burning.

SPECIAL LAMB ROAST SAUCE

(Mrs. Wm. G. Crawford)

⅓ cup Worcestershire
⅓ cup water
Dash salt

⅓ cup catsup
Juice of ½ lemon
1 teaspoon sugar

1. Mix all ingredients together and brush on lamb. While lamb is roasting baste every half hour with sauce.

BEARNAISE SAUCE

(Recipe Selection Committee)

½ cup vinegar
2 fresh tarragon leaves
4 tablespoons butter
Dash cayenne
2 tablespoons minced onions

4 beaten egg yolks
1 teaspoon chopped parsley
Dash salt
Dash pepper

1. Mix vinegar, tarragon leaves and onions. Bring to boil and cook for 5 minutes. Slowly add 4 beaten yolks, stirring constantly. Add butter a spoonful at a time, stirring well. Add salt, pepper, cayenne, parsley. Stir until well blended.

MUSHROOM SAUCE

(Recipe Selection Committee)

½ pound fresh mushrooms
¼ cup butter
¼ teaspoon salt
1 cup milk

¼ cup flour
½ teaspoon soy sauce (or Worcestershire)

1. Melt butter in saucepan. Add flour, mix well. Add milk. Stir until thick.
2. Slice mushrooms. Brown in butter until butter and mushrooms are brown. Add soy sauce. Add white sauce. Mix well.

NOTE: To be used over steaks, hamburgers or other meat dishes.

New River   Fort Lauderdale

NEW RIVER & GOVERNORS' CLUB, FORT LAUDERDALE, FLORIDA

Pickles and Relishes

Peter Piper picked a peck of pickled peppers; . . . .

Peter Piper
Nursery Rhyme
Anonymous

MANGO PICKLE

(Mrs. W. P. Brobeck, 1924
Woman's Club Cook Book)

1 quart hard sliced mangos
2 cups sugar
1 teaspoon ground cloves

1 pint vinegar
2 teaspoons cinnamon

1. Be sure to use hard mangos. Pare and slice as thick as possible.
2. Put vinegar, sugar, cinnamon and cloves in pan and bring to boil.
3. Pour hot mixture over sliced mangos and let stand one day.
4. Pour juice back into pan and bring to boil. Pour hot mixture over fruit and let stand another day.
5. Pour juice back into pan and bring to boil. Pour hot mixture over fruit and place in jars while still hot.

GREEN TOMATO ICEBERG PICKLES

(Mrs. Arthur W. Saarinen)

7 pounds medium sized green tomatoes
3 cups slack lime (household lime)
1 teaspoon ginger
1 teaspoon cinnamon

1 tablespoon celery seed
5 pounds sugar
3 pints vinegar
1 teaspoon allspice
1 teaspoon mace
1 tablespoon mustard seed

1. Wash tomatoes and slice thick leaving bud in end. To 2 gallons water add the lime, add tomatoes. Leave for 24 hours.
2. Drain tomatoes and wash each side of slice being careful not to break the slices. Soak 4 hours in clear water, changing water every hour. Drain.
3. Tie spices in bag. Put sugar, vinegar and spices in kettle. Bring to boil. Turn off heat. Drop in tomatoes and let stand overnight. Next day bring to boil and boil slowly for 1 hour.
4. Pack into sterile jars and seal.

GREEN PEPPER RELISH

(Mrs. Edward Heimburger, 1924
Woman's Club Cook Book)

12 red peppers	1 pint vinegar
12 green peppers	2 cups sugar
12 medium sized onions	1 tablespoon salt

1. Grind peppers and onions together. Drain.
2. Cover with boiling water and let stand 10 minutes. Drain.
3. Add vinegar, sugar and salt.
4. Bring to boil and boil for 15 minutes.
5. Seal in jars while hot.

FLAMINGO RELISH

(U. of Fla. Agr. Ext. Service
Bulletin 108A)

8 large white onions	2 cups sugar
12 large sweet red peppers	2 teaspoons mustard seed
2 hot peppers with seeds removed	2 teaspoons celery seed
	2 teaspoons salt
1 quart cider vinegar	

1. Remove skins from onions (be sure seeds are removed from hot peppers). Put onions, peppers through fine blade of food chopper.
2. Add vinegar, sugar, mustard seed, celery seed and salt, let stand 1 hour.
3. Bring mixture to boil and boil for 15 minutes.
4. Put into sterile jars and seal.

NOTE: May be used as catsup or instead of chili sauce.

TOMATO CATSUP

(Mrs. R. W. Burch, 1924
Woman's Club Cook Book)

1 peck ripe tomatoes, cut up
½ ounce allspice
¼ ounce ginger
4 ounces salt
1 pound brown sugar
2 or 3 red peppers, cut up

6 onions, cut up
½ ounce ground cloves
1 ounce black pepper
4 ounces dry mustard
1 quart vinegar

1. Put all ingredients into large pot and boil for 1½ hours.
2. Strain through sieve.
3. Store in sterilized bottles or jars.
4. When open, keep in refrigerator.

CHOW CHOW

(Mrs. Tom M. Bryan,
1917 So. Methodist Cook Book)

1 peck green tomatoes
1 dozen green peppers
3 small cabbages
½ cup horseradish
1 tablespoon dry mustard
1 teaspoon celery salt
½ peck ripe tomatoes
8 onions

3 red peppers
2 pounds brown sugar
1 tablespoon black pepper
1 tablespoon celery seed
1 teaspoon mace
Salt
Vinegar

1. Cut seeds out of green peppers. Grind peppers, tomatoes, onions, cabbages, red peppers together. Sprinkle with salt. Put into bag and allow to drain overnight.
2. In morning add sugar, horseradish, black pepper, mustard, celery seed, celery salt, mace and ground pepper-tomato mix.
3. Put into kettle. Cover with vinegar. Boil until clear.
4. Put into sterile jars and seal.

MANGO CHUTNEY (10 pints)

(Mrs. Henry O. Patton)

2 cups vinegar

2 quarts peeled and sliced ripe but firm mangos.

½ cup chopped green ginger root (or use crystallized)

2 large onions, sliced

½ teaspoon grated nutmeg

½ pound slivered almonds

6 cups sugar

4 chili peppers, chopped

2 cloves garlic, chopped

3 cups seedless raisins (1 package)

1 teaspoon salt

Juice of 2 medium sized limes

1. In large kettle boil vinegar and sugar for about 5 minutes. Add all other ingredients and simmer for about one hour or until fruit is tender.

2. Spoon into hot sterilized jars and seal.

GREEN MANGO CHUTNEY

(U. of Fla. Agr. Ext. Service Bulletin 108A)

4 pounds sliced and peeled green mangos

1 quart vinegar

2 pounds currants

2 pounds raisins

½ pound onions

3 pounds brown sugar

2 ounces yellow chili

½ pound green ginger

1 tablespoon salt

2 cloves garlic

1. Chop all ingredients fine except raisins and currants. These may be cut or left whole.

2. Mix chopped fruit, and all spices. Let stand overnight.

3. In morning bring to boil and cook until thick.

4. Put into sterile jars and seal.

TROPICAL CATSUP

(U. of Fla. Agr. Ext. Service
Bulletin 108A)

4 pounds prepared guavas
1 quart vinegar
1½ pounds raisins
¼ cup celery seed
1 teaspoon salt

1 clove garlic
2 tablespoons chilis or hot
  peppers
¼ cup mustard seed

1. Cut blossom and stem ends from guavas. If blemished, peel. Remove seed. Put guavas, raisins, garlic, ginger, mustard seed and chili through food chopper using fine blade. Add vinegar, sugar, salt. Bring to boil and boil for 30 minutes. Let stand overnight.
2. In morning if too thick, dilute with more vinegar. Heat to boiling point, put into sterile jars and seal.
3. Allow to stand for at least 2 weeks before using.

NOTE: Instead of guavas the following may be used: carissa, mangos, tamarinds.

PINK WATERMELON RELISH

(Recipe Selection Committee)

½ large watermelon
1 cup vinegar
4 tablespoons lime juice
12 whole cloves

2 cups sugar
1 lime sliced (2 small or 1 large)
1 stick cinnamon

1. Slice watermelon. Cut pink meat from rind. Cut into chunks. Place chunks in cheesecloth and squeeze to remove liquid. Pick out seeds.
2. Measure pulp (should be about 7 cups). Place in kettle. Add sugar, vinegar, cloves, cinnamon, lime juice and slices. Heat to boiling. Reduce heat and simmer for 30 minutes (or until thick and clear).
3. Pour into sterile jars and seal.
4. Store in cool dark place.

NOTE: Wonderful relish for main courses.

PINEAPPLE CHUTNEY RELISH

(U. of Fla. Agr. Ext. Service
Bulletin 108A)

1½ quarts shredded pineapple
12 large green mangos
 4 onions
 4 sweet red peppers
 2 hot red peppers
 6 medium sized green
   tomatoes
 1 cup cider vinegar

1 cup grape juice
2 cups brown sugar
Juice of 3 lemons or limes
¼ cup mustard seed
1 tablespoon ginger
2 cups raisins
1 tablespoon salt

1. Chop or grind the mangos (which have been peeled), onions, peppers, and tomatoes.
2. Add pineapple, vinegar, grape juice, brown sugar, lime juice, mustard seed, ginger, raisins and salt.
3. Cook until thick, stirring carefully from bottom of pan.
4. Put in sterile jars and seal.

SPICED WATERMELON RIND

(Recipe Selection Committee)

Rind from ½ large watermelon
½ cup salt
 1 sliced lime
 1 tablespoon allspice
 2 cups vinegar

8 cups water
4 cups sugar
12 whole cloves
 3 sticks cinnamon
 2 cups water

1. Pare skin from watermelon rind. Cut into 1 inch cubes (should be about 8 cups cubed rind).
2. Soak rind overnight in 8 cups water and salt. Drain.
3. Place in kettle, cover with water and bring to boil. Simmer for 10 minutes. Drain.
4. Combine sugar, cloves, allspice, vinegar and 2 cups water. Break cinnamon sticks in half and add to sugar mixture. Add sliced lime. Heat to boiling. Add cooked rind. Simmer, stirring from bottom of pan for 1 hour or until clear and syrup is thick.
5. Ladle into sterilized jars. Try to have piece of cinnamon and lime slice in each jar. Fill with the syrup and seal.

INLAND WATERWAY, FORT LAUDERDALE, FLORIDA

William D. King

Pies and Pastries

The Queen of Hearts
She made some tarts,
All on a summer's day; . . . .

The Queen of Hearts
Nursery Rhyme
Anonymous

KEY LIME PIE

(Mrs. Leslie Dunn)

1 9 inch graham cracker pie crust
1 can (16 ounce) condensed milk
½ teaspoon grated lime rind
½ cup lime juice
3 eggs
Dash salt

1. Make graham cracker crust holding out about 1 table-spoon of crumbs. Put pie plate in freezer.
2. Separate eggs. Mix yolks until thick. Add milk, rind and mix.
3. Gradually add lime juice to yolk mixture, stirring con-stantly.
4. Add pinch salt to egg whites and beat until stiff.
5. Fold egg whites into yolk mixture.
6. Pour mixture into pie shell and dribble the tablespoon of crumbs over top.
7. Put into freezer for at least 3 hours or may be left over night.

RUM KEY LIME PIE

(Mrs. Wm. F. Bigoney, Jr.)

9 inch graham cracker crust
¼ cup cold water
1 cup sugar
¼ cup rum
1 tablespoon unflavored gelatine
4 eggs
½ cup lime juice

1. Separate egg. Put yolks in top of double boiler and beat until thick. Mix ½ cup sugar and the lime juice and stir into yolks.
2. Cook over hot water stirring constantly until smooth and creamy.
3. Dissolve gelatine in cold water. Add to yolk mixture and stir until completely dissolved.
4. Remove from heat and cool mixture. Stir in rum.
5. Beat egg whites until stiff, beat in ½ cup sugar.
6. Fold whites into cooled yolk mixture.
7. Fill pie crust and chill in refrigerator at least 3 hours.

ANGEL KEY LIME PIE (makes 2)

(Mrs. Madeline C. Holdoway)

Meringue Shell: (for two 9 inch pie pans)

4 egg whites
1 cup sugar
½ teaspoon cream of tartar

1. Beat egg whites until frothy. Add cream of tartar, beat well then add sugar and beat until glossy (and you cannot feel grains of sugar when tasted).

2. Grease pie pans lightly and put meringue on bottom and sides of pan.

3. Bake at 275° for one hour. Turn oven off and leave in oven until dry (about ½ hour to 1 hour more).

Filling:

6 eggs
½ cup lime juice
12 tablespoons sugar
½ teaspoon lemon extract
1 can condensed milk (15 ounce)
½ teaspoon salt
1 teaspoon cream of tartar

1. Separate eggs. Beat yolks well, add milk and mix.

2. Add salt, then lime juice slowly, stirring constantly until the mixture thickens.

3. Beat egg whites until frothy. Add cream of tartar, beat, then add sugar, beating until glossy. Add extract.

4. Fold whites into yolk mixture.

5. Pour into baked meringue shells and place in freezer at least 3 hours.

6. May be served with whipped cream.

LIME MERINGUE PIE

(Mrs. Albert Frederick)

3 eggs
⅛ teaspoon salt
½ teaspoon grated lime rind

1 cup sugar
¼ cup lime juice
1 baked pie shell

1. Separate eggs. Beat yolks until thick. Add ½ cup sugar, salt, lime juice and rind. Mix well.

2. Cook in double boiler about 10 minutes, stirring, or until thickened. Remove from heat, cover and cool.

3. Beat egg whites until fluffy then beat in ½ cup sugar until sugar is completely dissolved.

4. Fold egg whites into cooled yolk mixture.

5. Pile into pie shell making swirls on top and bake about 10 minutes in 400° oven (or until honey brown).

Pie Shell:

1¼ cups sifted all purpose flour
7 tablespoons shortening

½ teaspoon salt
3 tablespoons water (approx.)

1. Sift flour and salt together.

2. Work in shortening until mixture is crumbly. Add only enough water to moisten. Mix and handle dough no more than absolutely necessary.

3. Roll dough out on floured board and cut to fit pie pan. Prick dough all over with fork to allow air to escape. Let dough stand in pan for 5 minutes to allow for shrinkage. Pat dough with ball of dough to work out all air.

4. Bake at 350° for about 10-15 minutes (or until brown).

CALAMONDIN PIE

(Mrs. W. E. Baughman)

To Make Calamondin Juice:

1. Cut calamondins in half. Press cut side down in sieve or strainer and work around until juice and pulp have been worked through, leaving skin and seeds. The pulp-juice can be used as is or can be further strained.

1 teaspoon unflavored gelatine	½ cup calamondin pulp-juice
2 eggs	1 tablespoon sugar
1 can condensed milk	1 baked pie shell

1. Put gelatin into calamondin juice and let dissolve.
2. Separate eggs. Beat yolks until thick with ½ tablespoon sugar. Add lime juice and condensed milk, stirring constantly.
3. Put mixture into pan and heat thoroughly.
4. Beat egg whites with ½ tablespoon sugar. Fold whites into calamondin mixture.
5. Pour into pie shell. Allow to set (can be put in refrigerator for about 4 hours). Grated calamondin rind can be sprinkled on top.

STRAWBERRY PIE

(Miss Emma Nelson)

1 baked pie shell	1 quart strawberries
1 cup sugar, approx.	1½ tablespoons corn starch
½ cup water	

1. Wash strawberries, remove cap and slice into at least 3 pieces each.
2. Put sliced strawberries in bowl and add sugar. Let stand several hours. Toss once or twice.
3. Drain juice.
4. Add cornstarch to water, mix well. Add juice and cook until clear and thick. Cool slightly.
5. Arrange sliced strawberries in pie shell. Pour cooked juice over berries.
6. Put in refrigerator at least 2-3 hours. Serve topped with whipped cream.

KEY LARGO ORANGE PIE FILLING

(Mrs. Robert S. Pendleton)

Filling:

2 cups orange juice
5 tablespoons corn starch
3 egg yolks
1 tablespoon butter
1 baked pie shell

1½ cups sugar
¼ cup water
½ teaspoon salt
3 tablespoons orange rind

1. Combine orange juice, sugar and bring to boil.
2. Mix cornstarch and water and add to orange juice mixture.
3. In double boiler put slightly beaten egg yolks, salt, butter and cook until thick. Add grated rind.
4. Combine yolk mixture with orange juice mixture, then pour into baked pie shell. Swirl topping over mixture.
5. Bake for about 15 minutes at 300°.

Topping:

3 egg whites
3 tablespoons ice water

6 tablespoons sugar
Pinch salt

1. Mix water and egg whites and beat until frothy. Add salt and slowly add sugar, beating until stiff.

COCONUT CUSTARD PIE

(Mrs. James F. Smalley)

3 eggs
1½ cups milk
1 cup shredded coconut
1 teaspoon lemon flavoring

½ cup sugar
¼ teaspoon salt
1 teaspoon vanilla
1 unbaked pie shell

1. Beat eggs. Add sugar, salt, milk, vanilla and lemon. Mix. Add coconut.
2. Pour into pie shell.
3. Bake for 15 minutes at 450°. Reduce temperature to 350° and bake for 30 more minutes.

COCONUT CREAM PIE

(Mrs. Albert Frederick)

1 baked pie crust
⅓ cup flour
3 eggs
1 cup fine grated coconut
2 cups milk (or 1 cup milk and 1 cup coconut milk)

⅞ cup sugar
⅛ teaspoon salt
1 teaspoon vanilla
6 tablespoons sugar

1. Mix sugar, flour, salt. Add milk.

2. Cook in double boiler until thickens.

3. Separate eggs. Add hot mixture to egg yolks a little at a time, stirring constantly.

4. Return mixture to stove and cook about 3 minutes longer.

5. Remove from stove, cover and cool. When cool, add vanilla and coconut.

6. Pour into baked pie shell.

7. Beat the egg whites until fluffy. Add dash salt. Add sugar slowly and continue beating until smooth and will peak.

8. Swirl meringue on pie and bake for about 15-20 minutes at 325°.

PECAN PIE

(Mrs. Richard Silvano)

1 unbaked 9 inch pie shell
1 cup sugar
¾ cup dark corn syrup
1 teaspoon vanilla
½ cup butter (1 stick)

3 eggs, slightly beaten
¼ teaspoon salt
1½ cups chopped pecans and some whole pecan meats

1. Chill pie shell for at least 4 hours. Do not prick shell.

2. Cream butter. Add sugar gradually and continue beating until light and fluffy.

3. Add eggs, syrup, salt, vanilla and chopped nuts.

4. Pour into pie shell.

5. Bake at 375° for 40-50 minutes.

6. Garnish with whole nuts.

SWEET POTATO PIE

(Mrs. A. W. Shackleford,
1917 So. Methodist Cook Book)

6 large sweet potatoes
2 eggs
Dash nutmeg

1 tablespoon butter
¼ cup milk
1 single pie crust, unbaked

1. Boil sweet potatoes until soft. Peel and mash.
2. Add butter, eggs and enough of the milk to soften mixture. Add nutmeg.
3. Bake in single pie crust at 350° for approx. 20 minutes or until set.

PECAN COOKIE PIE

(Mrs. Robert S. Pendleton)

Crust:

2 cups sifted flour
⅔ cup dark brown sugar

1 teaspoon baking powder
½ cup butter

1. Sift together the flour and baking powder. Stir in brown sugar. Cut in butter with fork or pastry blender. Mix will seem dry.
2. Pat evenly into bottom of well greased baking pan (size 11x7x1½ inches or 9x9x2 inches).
3. Bake for 15 minutes at 350°.

Filling:

½ cup dark brown sugar
4 eggs
1 teaspoon salt
¾ cup broken pecans

⅓ cup flour
1½ cups dark corn syrup
2 teaspoons vanilla

1. Mix sugar, flour. Beat eggs until well mixed. Add corn syrup. Mix into flour mixture. Add salt, vanilla. Mix well.
2. Pour over baked pie crust and sprinkle with nut meats.
3. Bake for 40 minutes at 350°. Cut into bars while warm.
4. Can be served with ice cream or whipped cream on top.

GRASSHOPPER PIE

(Mrs. Joseph A. Gore)

Crust:

1¼ cups crushed chocolate cookie wafers

⅓ cup melted butter

1. Pour melted butter over crushed wafers. Mix well. Press into 9 inch pie pan and chill at least 1 hour.

Filling:

⅔ cup scalded milk
24 marshmallows
½ pint whipping cream

2 ounces green creme de menthe
1 ounce white creme de cocoa

1. Add marshmallows to scalded milk and melt in top of double boiler stirring often. Cool to room temperature. Add creme de menthe and creme de cocoa.

2. Whip cream. Fold into marshmallow mixture. Pour into crust.

3. Put into deep freeze (at least 3 hours).

4. May be served with whipped cream on top.

CHESS PIE

(Mrs. Mary Emma Warriner)

1 cup sugar
1 stick butter
1 teaspoon vanilla

3 eggs
1 pinch salt

1. Mix sugar and softened (not melted) butter. Add vanilla.
2. Stir eggs into mixture.
3. Pour into unbaked pie shell. Bake for 15 - 20 minutes at 350° or until just brown.
4. Leave pie in oven and turn off heat. Keep in oven until just firm.
5. May be served with spoon of currant jelly or preserves on top.

GREEN MANGO PIE

(Mrs. Alfred J. Beck)

1 9 inch unbaked pastry shell
2 tablespoons fresh ground
   ginger (or pulverized or
   candied)

½ stick butter
1 cup sugar
1 teaspoon nutmeg
Green mangos

1. Select mangos that are mature but still green. Peel and slice **very thin.** Should have about 3 cups sliced mango.
2. Mix butter and sugar. Add nutmeg and ginger.
3. Pile mango slices in unbaked pie shell. Spread butter mix over mangos. Put crust on top. Prick top crust with fork.
4. Bake for 30 minutes at 350°, reduce heat to 250° and bake for 30 more minutes.
5. Serve warm with hard sauce or with whipped cream.

NOTE: See index for Pie Shell Pastry.

FRESH ROSELLE TARTS

(Mrs. Ann M. Perry)

2 cups sugar
1 tablespoon flour
¼ teaspoon salt
½ teaspoon allspice
⅓ cup water

4 cups roselle calyces
½ lemon rind, grated
2 tablespoons butter
½ cup walnuts meats, chopped
Pastry for a 10 inch pie

1. Mix sugar, flour, allspice and salt. Add water and heat until sugar is dissolved.
2. Add roselle and cook until tender. Add lemon rind and butter.
3. Pour half the mixture into pastry lined 10 inch pie plate. Sprinkle with nuts and add remaining mixture. Top with pastry strips placed lattice-wise.
4. Bake for 30 minutes in oven at 425°.

BEST EVER PIE

(Mrs. Vernon Maxwell)

2 eggs	1 cup sugar
1 teaspoon cinnamon	1 teaspoon cloves
½ cup pecan halves	½ cup seedless raisins
1 tablespoon melted butter	1 tablespoon vinegar
1 unbaked 8 inch pie shell	

1. Separate eggs. Beat yolks until thick. Add sugar, cinnamon, cloves, pecans, raisins and butter.
2. Beat egg whites until stiff. Fold into mixture and as you are folding add the vinegar.
3. Pour into pie shell.
4. Bake at 450° for 10 minutes, reduce heat to 350° and bake for 25 minutes more.

ORANGE CREME PUFFS (8 - 10)

(Mrs. Mary Tsolas)

10 baked Creme Puffs	1½ cups orange juice
1 tablespoon lemon juice	½ cup sugar
3 tablespoons flour	⅛ teaspoon salt
2 teaspoons grated orange rind	2 egg yolks
2 tablespoons butter	½ pint heavy cream
1 tablespoon sugar	

1. In saucepan put orange juice, lemon juice and bring to boil. Add sugar, flour, salt. Stir until thick. Add rind, egg yolks, butter, stirring well. Cook until blended. Chill.
2. Beat cream until thick, add 1 tablespoon sugar, blend. Fold cream into chilled orange mixture.
3. Split creme puffs. Pile orange creme into shells. Put top back on and glaze with Orange Glaze.

RICE CRISPIE PIE

(Mrs. James D. Camp, Jr.)

3 cups Rice Crispies
2 tablespoons butter

1 package sweet chocolate chips
Ice cream

1. Melt butter and chocolate in pan. Add Rice Crispies and press into pie pan.
2. Fill up pie shell with peppermint ice cream and put in freezer.

CHOCOLATE-CHOCOLATE PIE

(Mrs. R. H. Gore, Jr.)

1/3 cup thin chocolate wafer crumbs
1/4 teaspoon cinnamon
4 egg whites
1/4 teaspoon cream of tartar

1 cup semi-sweet chocolate chips (or grated chocolate bar)
1 cup sugar
1 pint heavy cream

1. Mix chocolate wafer crumbs, cinnamon. Beat egg whites until stiff but not dry. Slowly add sugar, cream of tartar. Beat until stiff and glossy. Fold crumbs into whites.
2. Spread over bottom and sides of well buttered 9 inch pie tin. Make bottom about 1/2 inch thick and sides about 2 inches thick. Do not cover rim.
3. Bake about 1 hour at 275° or until crust is brown and crisp. Cool away from drafts. The meringue will crack and the center will fall on cooling, this makes room for filling.
4. **Filling:** Fill center with whipped cream to which you have added 1 teaspoon sugar and 1 teaspoon vanilla. Put layer of whipped cream and layer of chocolate chips. Chill thoroughly.

PECAN ICE BOX PIE

(Mrs. M. R. Hunter)

20 soda crackers
4 egg whites

1 cup sugar
1 cup pecan meats, chopped

1. Crush crackers making fine crumbs. Add ½ cup sugar and nut meats. Mix well.
2. Beat egg whites stiff. Add ½ cup sugar and beat well.
3. Mix crumb mixture with egg whites. Pile into well buttered pie pan.
4. Bake for 30 minutes at 350° (or until mixture is brown). Cool.
5. Place in refrigerator for at least 2 hours. Serve with whipped cream.

PUMPKIN CHIFFON PIE

(Mrs. Oscar P. Pearson)

1 9 inch deep baked pie shell
½ cup brown sugar
½ teaspoon nutmeg
¼ teaspoon ginger
1 cup evaporated milk
1¼ cups cooked pumpkin

1 envelope unflavored gelatine
½ teaspoon salt
½ teaspoon cinnamon
2 eggs
½ cup cold water

1. Separate eggs. In top of double boiler beat egg yolks. Add milk, pumpkin.
2. Soften gelatin in water, add to yolk mixture. Add ¼ cup brown sugar, salt, nutmeg, cinnamon, ginger.
3. Cook about 10 minutes, stirring. Cool, stirring once in a while. Refrigerate until thick but not set (about 1 hour).
4. Beat egg whites until foamy. Slowly beat in ¼ cup brown sugar. Beat until stiff.
5. Fold pumpkin mixture into egg whites. Pour into baked pie shell. Chill until set (about 4 hours).
6. Top with whipped cream when serving.

CREME PUFFS (12 large)

(Mrs. Richard Silvano)

1 cup water
½ cup butter (1 stick)
4 eggs

1 cup flour
¼ teaspoon salt

1. Put water, butter, salt in pan. Heat to boiling.
2. Add all flour at once and stir vigorously until the mixture no longer clings to side of pan.
3. Remove from heat and cool slightly.
4. Add eggs one at a time, beating vigorously after each egg is added.
5. Divide mixture into 12 parts. Drop onto a well buttered baking sheet about 2 inches apart.
6. Bake in 450° oven for 20 minutes. Reduce heat to 325° for 20 minutes longer.
7. Cool, cut slit in side and fill. Use favorite filling, cream, pudding, shrimp, crab, tuna, etc.

GRAHAM CRACKER CRUST

(Recipe Selection Committee)

1¼ cups rolled graham cracker crumbs

2 tablespoons sugar
¾ stick butter (6 tablespoons)

1. Melt butter completely in pan.
2. Mix sugar with crumbs.
3. Mix crumbs thoroughly into butter-mix.
4. Press onto bottom and sides of 9 inch pie pan.
5. Can be chilled or baked:
   (1) If baked, put pan in oven for 7 minutes at 375°. Now ready for filling.
   (2) If chilled, put into refrigerator or freezer for at least one hour before using.

PIE SHELL PASTRY (5 pies)

(Mrs. Mary Emma Warriner)

5½ cups flour
  1 tablespoon salt
Water

1 pound lard
1 egg

1. Put flour into large bowl and cut in lard until crumbly.
2. Put egg into measuring cup and fill cup to one cup level with water. Mix well.
3. Add egg-water to flour and mix.
4. Wrap in foil and put in refrigerator (will keep three weeks). Or put into deep freeze (will keep indefinitely).
5. When needed, take out a portion. Let warm up to room temperature (or until pliable). Roll out on floured board.

NOTE: For storing, divide into five balls and wrap each in foil or in plastic bag.

~~~~~~~~~~~~~~~~

SHORT PIE CRUST

(Mrs. John P. Pearson)

1 cup biscuit mix
¼ cup soft lard

3 tablespoons boiling water

1. Put biscuit mix and lard into 9 inch pie plate. Add boiling water and stir vigorously to form a ball that cleans the pan (fork best for this). Dough will be puffy and soft.
2. With fingers flatten dough in center of plate and pat evenly up the sides to form a shell. Prick with fork.
3. Bake at 450° for about 8 - 10 minutes.

NOTE: This is real tender and crumbly kind of crust. Use only with a filling that does not have to be re-baked.

THE BEACH AT FORT LAUDERDALE, FLORIDA

Poultry and Game

A chicken in every pot . . . .

Political Campaign Slogan

1932

GAME

There are many ways to prepare our local game. Our list is just to be used as a guide.

DEER — clean as soon as possible. Remove insides, head, feet, tail and skin. Hang at least a week or two before using. Should be marinated 24 hours before cooking. May be used in many ways, roasts, steaks, stews.

DOVE — clean as soon as possible. Remove insides, head, feet and feathers. May be boiled, broiled, roasted, used in pies.

DUCK (WILD) — clean as soon as possible. Remove insides, head, feet and feathers. Soak in salt water or soda water to help remove gamey taste. Use regular duck recipes, except for stuffing. Put quartered apple, onion and celery inside and discard before serving. Strips of bacon or pork fat across breast when roasting help.

GOOSE (WILD) — see Wild Duck.

OPOSSUM — clean as soon as possible. Scald using ½ cup dry lime (or lye) to 1 gallon boiling water. Scald quickly. Pull off hair at once. Scrape well. Cut off head, feet, tail, remove insides. Clean thoroughly in fresh hot water. Soak overnight in pan of cold salted water (½ cup salt to pan of water).

QUAIL — clean as soon as possible. Remove insides, head, feet and feathers. May be roasted, broiled.

RABBIT (WILD) — clean as soon as possible. Remove insides, head, feet and skin. Wipe with cloth dipped in hot water to remove loose hair. Soak in vinegar water for 12-24 hours. Use any rabbit recipe.

RACOON — clean as soon as possible. Remove head, tail, feet, insides and skin. Should be hung for at least 24 hours before using. Parboil, then roast.

SQUIRREL — clean as soon as possible. Remove head, feet, tail, insides and skin. May be used in many ways, boiled, fried, stews, roasts.

TURKEY (WILD) — see Wild Duck.

CURRIED CHICKEN

(Mrs. Wm. C. Knox,
Pachira Garden Club)

4 cups coconut milk
1 large Spanish onion, minced
4 tablespoons chopped ginger root
6 tablespoons flour
4 tablespoons curry
3 cups chicken breast, diced
8 peppercorns
½ teaspoon celery salt

Pinch thyme
½ cup butter
1 clove garlic, crushed
1 teaspoon cinnamon
4 teaspoons sugar
3 whole cloves
1 teaspoon salt
2 tablespoons curry
2 slightly beaten egg yolks

1. Cook onion in butter until transparent. Add ginger, garlic, cinnamon, 4 tablespoons curry and sugar. Add flour. Stir in coconut milk, cook 5 minutes or until thick. Place over boiling water for 45 minutes. If sauce is not thick enough, use egg yolks.
2. Place uncooked chicken breasts in pot. Cover with water. Add cloves, peppercorns, salt, celery salt, 2 tablespoons curry and pinch of thyme. Cook until tender.
3. Remove chicken from water. Dice meat to make 3 cups. Add chicken to curry sauce and serve over rice.

BUTTERFLY CHICKEN

(Mrs. Arch Campbell)

2 whole fryer chickens (2½-3 pounds each)
1 tablespoon salt
1 teaspoon fresh ground pepper

Optional seasonings: 4 garlic cloves, coarsely chopped, or rosemary or marjoram
1 cup olive oil

1. Halve chicken only through breast side leaving together at backbone. Press open.
2. Rub chicken with salt, pepper and spice (garlic or rosemary or marjoram).
3. Place chicken, skin side down in baking pan. Pour olive oil over chicken.
4. Fry over high heat until golden brown on skin side only.
5. Preheat oven to 450°. Put pan of chicken in oven and bake 15 minutes. Turn chicken, basting with olive oil and bake another 15 minutes, or until skin is crunchy.

DOVE PIE (serves 6)

(Mrs. Mark Liner)

8-10 doves
1 cup diced potato
¼ cup chopped celery
½ cup cooked peas
1 bay leaf

2 cups water
½ cup sliced carrots
¼ cup chopped onion
Dash parsley
Dash thyme

1. Clean doves, remove feathers, head, intestines and feet. Leave doves whole.
2. Put doves in deep well or large kettle and add water (enough to cover). Salt and pepper to taste.
3. Simmer doves until almost tender (about 45 minutes).
4. Add raw potatoes, carrots, celery, onion, cooked peas, parsley, bay leaf and thyme.
5. Cover and simmer until vegetables are tender (about 30 minutes).
6. Remove doves and vegetables, and place in ungreased baking dish.
7. Thicken stock, using proportions of 1 cup stock and 1 tablespoon of flour. Pour this over doves and vegetables.
8. Cover top with biscuit topping and bake 20-25 minutes in 425° oven or until topping is browned.

FOWL STUFFED WITH RICE AND GREEN GRAPES

(Mrs. Curtis D. Benton, Jr.)

1 roasting fowl, cleaned
½ medium onion, chopped
1 cup chicken broth
1 tablespoon butter

½ cup chopped celery
1 cup uncooked rice
1 cup seedless green grapes

1. Wash and dry fowl. Rub with salt and pepper on inside.
2. Melt butter in pan. Cook celery and onions until transparent. Remove celery and onions from pan.
3. Put rice in pan and brown. Add chicken broth. Add celery, onions and green grapes. Mix well.
4. Stuff fowl with mixture. Truss.
5. Bake for about 1½ hours at 325° or until fowl is brown. Baste with juices.

CHICKEN AND EGGBREAD (serves 4)

(Mrs. Gilbert B. Dickey, Jr.)

Chicken:

1. In large covered pot, boil two 3 to 4 pound chickens in salted water until tender.

2. Take white meat from bones (save dark meat for other dishes). Save the broth.

Sauce:

3 tablespoons butter	1 small onion chopped fine
1 small green pepper minced	1½ cups chicken broth
1½ cups whipping cream	½ teaspoon paprika
1 tablespoon chopped parsley	1 large can sliced mushrooms
3 tablespoons flour	Salt

1. Add flour to cooled chicken broth and salt to taste.

2. Melt butter in pan and saute onion, pepper. Do not brown.

3. Add broth and cream, mushrooms, parsley, paprika.

4. Cook until consistency of thick white sauce.

To Serve:

1. Make eggbread. Cut eggbread into four equal squares. Cut each square in half, making two layers.

2. Place bottom half on serving dish. Heap thick slices of white chicken meat on bottom, put on top piece.

3. Spoon sauce over top, add sprig of parsley and serve immediately.

NOTE: See Index for Eggbread recipe. A real party dish. Finish meal with a fruit salad, hot coffee.

CHICKEN VENEZIA

(Mrs. Will Rodgers)

1 8 ounce package green
  noodles
1 envelope Italian style
  spaghetti sauce mix
1 6 ounce can tomato paste
1 4 ounce can mushrooms
1 small can ripe olives

¼ cup grated cheese
1¾ cups water
1 teaspoon bitters
2 tablespoons oil
3 cups diced cooked chicken
1 6 ounce can pimiento
1 pint sour cream

1. Cook green noodles in boiling salted water until tender, drain.
2. Combine spaghetti sauce mix, water, bitters, tomato paste and oil.
3. Bring to boil, reduce heat and simmer 10 minutes.
4. Add mushrooms (including liquid), chicken, olives, pimiento which has been cut into strips.
5. Arrange green noodles around bottom and sides of greased 2 quart casserole dish. Pour sauce into middle and over noodles.
6. Sprinkle top with cheese.
7. Bake 20 to 25 minutes at 375°.
8. Just before serving, fold in sour cream.

WILD DUCK

(Recipe Selection Committee)

Follow favorite recipe for duck except if roasting duck, do not use stuffing. Fill cavity with quartered apple, onion and stalk of celery if room enough. Discard apple, onion and celery before serving. If the duck is old or very heavy, duck should be soaked for about 1 hour in soda water (1 tablespoon soda to kettle of water) before roasting.

TURKEY ALMOND CHOW MEIN

(Mrs. Walter B. Hilliard,
Pachira Garden Club)

½ cup sliced mushrooms
½ cup blanched almonds
3 tablespoons salad oil
1 clove garlic, cut in half
1 teaspoon salt
1 cup diced bamboo shoots
½ cup thinly-sliced water chestnuts
½ cup thinly-sliced celery
1 cup diced cold turkey

1 tablespoon liquid from bamboo shoots
1 tablespoon liquid from water chestnuts
2 tablespoons cornstarch
2 tablespoons bead molasses
2 tablespoons soy sauce
½ teaspoon sugar
⅓ cup sliced green onions
4 tablespoons water

1. Brown almonds in 1 tablespoon oil. Set aside.

2. With fork, mash garlic into salt in skillet.

3. Add 1 tablespoon oil, then add turkey.

4. Brown slightly.

5. Add remaining tablespoon oil, then add bamboo shoots, mushrooms and brown lightly.

6. Add 2 tablespoons liquid.

7. Cover tightly.

8. Cook over low heat for 5 minutes.

9. Add water chestnuts, celery and half of the slivered almonds.

10. Just heat through. Celery and chestnuts should remain crisp.

11. For gravy, shake up in small jar the cornstarch, sugar, water and soy sauce with the bead molasses. Stir into turkey mixture.

12. Cook until liquid thickens, and serve over Chinese noodles.

13. Sprinkle top of dish with the sliced green onions and remainder of the almonds.

MANDARIN DUCK FRICASSEE (serves 6)

(Recipe Selection Committee)

1 duck (5-6 pounds cut up)
1 tablespoon sugar
1 tablespoon chopped candied ginger
2 cups water
2 tablespoons cornstarch
2 cups mandarin orange sections (regular orange or tangerine sections may be used)

¼ cup soy sauce
½ teaspoon salt
1 clove garlic
¼ cup salad oil
1 cup orange juice
¼ cup water

1. Mix soy, sugar, salt and ginger. Place duck in marinade, and leave for at least two hours (overnight is better).

2. Heat oil in pan, add garlic (sliced or mashed) and saute duck until brown. Pour in orange juice and water. Cover and simmer about 2 hours or until duck is tender.

3. Lift duck out of pan and place on heated pan in oven (just to keep warm).

4. Mix cornstarch in ¼ cup cold water. Pour into juice duck was cooked in. Add orange sections and cook for about 5 more minutes.

5. Put duck on serving platter and pour orange mixture over duck. Serve at once.

NOTE: Wonderful with wild rice.

WILD TURKEY

(Recipe Selection Committee)

Follow favorite recipe for turkey except if roasting, fill cavity with quartered apples, onions and celery. Discard after roasting. Some prefer to soak the bird before roasting to help remove some of the gamy flavor (soak for one hour in kettle of water which has 1 tablespoon soda added).

OLD FASHIONED CHICKEN AND DUMPLINGS

(Mrs. Mary Latshaw by
(Mrs. Harry H. Smith)

Chicken:

1 fat hen cut into pieces
1 small onion

1½ teaspoons salt
Few celery leaves, cut up

1. Put hen pieces in kettle, cover with water, add small onion cut up, few celery leaves and salt. Bring to boil and reduce heat. Cook until done (2-4 hours depending on size).
2. Lift out pieces of chicken. Reserve all broth. If quantity is greatly reduced, add little more water. Bring back to boil.

Dumplings:

3 cups flour
1 egg
1 teaspoon salt

1½ cups boiling broth with fat in broth

1. Mix flour and salt. Make a well in flour. Pour boiling broth with fat into well. Mix and cool.
2. When cool, mix in slightly beaten egg.
3. Roll on floured board. Cut into strips 1 inch wide and 2 inches long.
4. Into boiling broth in kettle, drop dumplings a few at a time. Cover and boil for 20 minutes. Watch or it will boil over.
5. Add chicken to reheat. Add a little water if dry. Serve.

FRIED QUAIL

(Recipe Selection Committee)

1 quail per person
Hot cooking oil

Flour
Salt and pepper to taste

1. Dip cleaned quail in seasoned flour to coat well.
2. In deep fryer, heat cooking oil until hot (should have pan about half full of oil).
3. Fry quail, turning to brown on all sides. Reduce heat and cook until tender, about 20 minutes. Drain on paper towel and serve at once.

CHICKEN-SPAGHETTI CROQUETTES

(Mrs. Louella Snyder)

1½ cups chopped cold chicken
½ cup chopped cooked mushrooms
2 tablespoons water
1 cup thick white sauce
Dash nutmeg

½ cup chopped cooked spaghetti
2 tablespoons chopped celery
1 egg
¾ cup fine bread crumbs

1. Put chicken through meat grinder. Add spaghetti, mushrooms, celery, nutmeg, hot Thick White Sauce and mix well.
2. Chill mixture. Form into croquettes.
3. Slightly beat egg with 2 tablespoons of water.
4. Roll croquettes in bread crumbs, in egg batter, then in crumbs again.
5. Fry in hot fat until brown.

Thick White Sauce:
2 tablespoons butter
1 cup milk
Dash pepper

4 tablespoons flour
½ teaspoon salt

1. Melt butter, add flour and mix.
2. Add salt, pepper and milk stirring constantly.
3. Bring to boil.
4. Place pan over hot water until ready to use.

ROAST QUAIL (serves 4)

(Recipe Selection Committee)

4 cleaned quail
Butter
Salt and pepper to taste

4 slices bacon
1 tablespoon sherry or lime juice

1. Wash and dry quail. Rub inside and outside with salt and pepper. Brush with butter. Wrap each quail in strip of bacon and fasten with toothpick. Place on roasting pan.
2. Bake at 350° for 45 - 60 minutes. Baste with a mixture of 1 tablespoon melted butter and 1 tablespoon sherry (or lime juice). When golden brown, remove from oven.
3. If juice in bottom of pan, pour over quail. If not enough juice, add little more butter, sherry and heat.

ROAST DUCK WITH PINEAPPLE RICE DRESSING

(Recipe Selection Committee)

1 cleaned drawn duck (4-5 pounds)

2 cups Dressing

1. Wash duck under running water. Pat dry with paper towel. Stuff duck (neck cavity and body). Lace. Do not pack dressing in tight. Do not tie legs tightly to body.
2. Place duck on rack, breast side up. Do not add water, do not baste, do not prick skin.
3. Bake for about 2 hours at 325°.

Dressing:

½ cup uncooked rice
1 stalk celery with top
1 small can crushed pineapple
Dash salt
Dash pepper

1 small onion
Sprigs parsley
2 tablespoons butter
Dash thyme

1. Cook rice according to package. Melt butter. Add chopped onion, celery and cook until tender. Add drained pineapple, parsley, salt, pepper, thyme and rice. Mix well. Stuff duck.

BARBECUE QUAIL

(Recipe Selection Committee)

6-8 quail
Deep fat

4 cups barbecue sauce

1. Have quail dressed. Split down back.
2. In fry pan heat deep fat. Brown quail. Pour off all fat.
3. Add barbecue sauce to quail. Simmer for about 2 hours or until quail are tender. Baste often with sauce. Turn quail several times.

NOTE: See index for Barbecue Sauce recipe.

WILD GOOSE

(Recipe Selection Committee)

Follow favorite recipe for goose except if roasting, fill cavity with quartered apple, onion and celery. Discard after roasting. To help remove some of the gamy flavor, soak goose for one hour in soda water (1 tablespoon soda to kettle of water).

ROAST GOOSE

(Recipe Selection Committee)

1. Use 8-10 pound goose. Stuff and truss.
2. Place on back on rack in roasting pan. Prick skin several times.
3. Roast at 325° for 25 minutes per pound.

NOTE: Regular bread stuffing can be used but many prefer to place quartered apple, stalk of celery and quartered onion in cavity, and discard after roasting.

HASENPFEFFER

(Recipe Selection Committee)

1 rabbit	3 cloves
Vinegar and water	1 bay leaf
1 sliced onion	1 cup thick sour cream
Salt and pepper to taste	Butter

1. Cut rabbit up. Wash and put in pan. Cover with vinegar-water mix (half vinegar to half water). Add onion, cloves, bay leaf, salt and pepper. Let soak for 2 days (or if using domestic rabbit, just overnight). Remove rabbit. Dry.
2. In frying pan, melt butter, and brown rabbit on all sides quickly.
3. Pour the soaking juice over the rabbit just to cover. Cover pan and simmer about 45 minutes, or until tender.
4. Just before serving mix in sour cream.

CASSEROLE OF RABBIT (serves 4)

(Fort Lauderdale Daily News,
December 10, 1925)

1 cut up rabbit
Flour
Salt and pepper to taste
1 cup diced tart apple
½ cup diced celery

1 whole onion
2 tablespoons minced onion
1 cup diced carrot
Water
Cooking oil
Biscuit topping may be used if desired

1. Put cut up rabbit in pot. Cover with salted water and let stand overnight. Remove rabbit and throw out water.
2. Put rabbit in kettle. Cover with water. Add whole onion. Bring to boil. Cook for 30 minutes. Remove rabbit and throw out water and onion.
3. In dish mix some flour, salt and pepper. Dredge rabbit in flour.
4. In frying pan, heat cooking oil. When hot, add rabbit. Brown on all sides. Remove rabbit.
5. Put rabbit in casserole dish. Add minced onions, carrots, apple and celery.
6. Make a thin gravy out of the frying pan oil. Pour over the rabbit and vegetables. Cover the casserole.
7. Bake for 1 hour in 350° oven.
8. If topping desired, remove dish from oven. Put biscuit topping on hot rabbit and vegetables. Check to see if there is still some liquid in casserole. If too dry, add ¼ cup water. Put casserole back into oven for 15 minutes at 375° or until biscuit topping is brown.

ROAST VENISON

(Recipe Selection Committee)

Roast of venison

½ pound salt pork or bacon

1. Place strips of salt pork or bacon across top of roast.
2. Roast uncovered at 325° for 35 - 45 minutes per pound.

RACOON

(Robert S. Pendleton)

1. Soak coon overnight in salted water (½ cup salt to pot of water). Drain.
2. Place coon in fresh water to which a few favorite spices have been added (1 teaspoon salt, lime juice, rosemary, sage, basil, etc.). Bring to a boil and cook for 1 hour. Drain.
3. Stuff cavity with corn bread stuffing. Wrap in foil.
4. Bake for about 2 hours at 350°.

VENISON STEAKS

(1917 So. Methodist Cook Book)

1. Cut venison into slices about ½ inch thick.
2. Season with salt, pepper and flour.
3. Cook in deep fat in covered pan until done.
4. Remove to hot platter, butter, and serve immediately.

BROILED SQUIRREL (serves 4)

(Recipe Selection Committee)

2 cleaned squirrels
Cooking oil

Salt and pepper to taste
2 tablespoons lemon or lime juice

1. Rub squirrels with salt and pepper. Brush with cooking oil.
2. Place under broiler for about 40 minutes total time. Every 10 minutes, brush squirrels with drippings, and turn.
3. Use pan drippings to make gravy, thicken with flour, and add 2 tablespoons lemon or lime juice.

ROAST PHEASANT

(Recipe Selection Committee)

1 pheasant
2 teaspoons pepper
1 medium onion
1 apple

2 tablespoons salt
2 stalks celery
4 strips bacon
1 cup water

1. Clean pheasant. Sprinkle salt and pepper into cavity. Quarter apple, quarter onion and put into cavity. Cut celery stalks in half. Put celery into cavity.
2. Sprinkle salt and pepper over breast and skin of pheasant. Lay strips of bacon over breast.
3. Put pheasant on rack in roasting pan. Put 1 cup water in bottom of pan.
4. Roast for about 2½ hours at 350° or until tender. Baste several times while roasting.

MAKE-AHEAD DRESSING (for two 20-24 pound turkeys)

(Mrs. Thomas J. Newbill)

1½ quarts ground onion (or 6 bags chopped frozen)
1 full bunch parsley
2 large loaves bread, cubed and toasted
2 cans beef gravy (chicken gravy may be used)

1½ quarts chopped pascal celery, tops removed
1 pan cornbread
2 cans condensed mushroom soup
4 small cans chopped black olives
Assorted spices

1. In blender with a little water, blend parsley and celery tops.
2. In large pot cook onions, celery and parsly-celery mix with just enough liquid to cover. Add favorite family spices (such as rosemary, thyme, savory, sage and basil).
3. Crumble cornbread. Mix with toasted bread cubes. Add to spice mixture. Add olives, soup and gravy. Mix well.

NOTE: Can be divided and frozen for use at a later date.

MOTHER'S DRESSING (1 quart)

(Mrs. Wm. G. Crawford)

2 cups stale white bread crumbs
4 medium onions, chopped
1 tablespoon sugar
3 eggs
2 cups Eggbread

5 stalks celery, chopped
¼ teaspoon pepper
Chicken or turkey broth
⅓ cup cooking oil

1. Put oil in frying pan. Add onions, celery and cook until tender.
2. Crumble two breads together. Add celery-onion mixture. Add sugar, pepper and 3 slightly beaten eggs. Mix well. If mixture is too dry, moisten by adding a little chicken or turkey broth.
3. Use to stuff bird.
4. If cooking in separate pan, add enough broth to make bread mixture pour. Pour into baking dish at least 3 inches deep.
5. Bake about 1 hour at 350°.
6. Serve with giblet gravy over dressing.

Giblet Gravy:

1. Put giblets in saucepan. Cover with water. Add dash salt, pepper. Bring to boil. Simmer until tender. Remove giblets.
2. Add 4 - 6 tablespoons flour to ¼ cup cold water. Mix. Stir into giblet broth.
3. Add about 1 cup of drippings from roast turkey. Mix well. Bring gravy to boil, reduce heat and simmer for 5 minutes.
4. Chop giblets. Add to gravy.

NOTE: See index for Eggbread recipe.

OYSTER DRESSING

(1917 So. Methodist Cook Book)

3 cups stale bread crumbs
Dash salt
Dash pepper

1 pint oysters
½ cup melted butter
½ teaspoon onion juice

1. Mix butter, bread crumbs, salt, pepper and onion juice.
2. Drain oysters. Check for shell bits. Stir into bread crumb mixture.

NOTE: This is used to stuff turkey or chicken.

OPOSSUM

(Mike Morgan)

Prepare opossum as you would prepare a suckling pig. (See Game List for preparation).

Make a stuffing of:

1 tablespoon butter
1 large onion, chopped
Opossum liver (optional)
1 cup bread crumbs
1 red pepper, chopped

1 hard boiled egg
1 teaspoon salt
Dash Worcestershire
Water to moisten

1. Melt butter in frying pan. Add onion. Brown. Add finely chopped liver (if desired) and cook until tender and well done. Add bread crumbs, red pepper, Worcestershire, chopped hard boiled egg, salt. Add enough water to moisten.

2. Stuff opossum. Sew opening or fasten with skewers. Place in roaster. Add two tablespoons water. Put in uncovered roasting pan.

3. Roast at 350° until very tender and richly brown (about 1½ - 2 hours). Baste every 15 minutes with drippings.

4. Remove from oven. Remove stiches. Place opossum on heated platter.

5. Skim fat from gravy in pan. Serve gravy separately.

6. If head has been left on, place a red apple or baked sweet potato in the mouth.

7. If no opossums are available, serve the red apple or baked sweet potato.

NOTE: Opossums are not easy to come by at the meat market, but you never can tell when you might run over one some dark night and need the above recipe. This is my favorite opossum recipe which I shall some day try if donated a prepared opossum and a cook.

OLD FEDERAL HIGHWAY BRIDGE, FORT LAUDERDALE, FLORIDA

Salads and Dressings

Lettuce is like conversation: it must be fresh and crisp,
so sparkling that you scarcely notice the bitter in it.

My Summer in a Garden
Charles Dudley Warner
(1829-1900)

HEARTS OF PALM SALAD (serves 8 to 10)

(Philip Weidling)

For the neophyte the preparation of hearts of palm salad from the raw materials presents a formidable task. If properly done, however, the result is a gourmet dish well worth the effort.

The raw materials include a bowl of cracked ice or ice cubes, mayonnaise and a palm heart stump. The latter will be two to three feet long and three to four inches in diameter. It is made up, actually, of the unborn leaves, or fronds, of the palm tree, plus an outside covering of the base of leaves that have already spread.

The lower end of the stump will have a pulpy pith which is not used. It will be observed that each leaf, as it is peeled off will have a thin side and thick side. The thin side can easily be cut with a knife and the leaf peeled off. As you progress toward the center of the stump you will find the lower end, next to the pulp, is snowy white. This is the good part. It can be tested by simply breaking in your fingers. If it breaks easily, it is tender and good.

Ingredients:

1 Palm Heart Stump   Mayonnaise

1 bowl ice cubes or cracked ice   Paprika

1. After heart is peeled, drop immediately into cracked ice to prevent turning brown.

2. Grate or finely slice heart. Mix with mayonnaise. Add a dash of paprika for color.

NOTE: Salad can be mixed with shrimp or crab meat to make a main course dish.

EMERALD SALAD (serves 8)

(Mrs. Curtis G. Pratt)

1 package lime Jello
1 medium cucumber, diced
1 cup creamed cottage cheese
1 cup sliced almonds
½ teaspoon Accent

¾ cup hot water
1 medium onion, diced
1 cup mayonnaise
1 teaspoon dried horseradish
2 drops green coloring

1. Dissolve lime Jello in ¾ cup boiling water. Cool until partially congealed. Add cucumber, onion, cottage cheese, mayonnaise, almonds, Accent. Mix well. If wanted a deeper green color, add green coloring. Mix well.
2. Chill thoroughly in refrigerator.

~~~~~~~~~~~~~~~~~~~~

FRUIT SALAD, MOLDED

(Mrs. Tom M. Bryan)

1 package lime Jello
1 cup boiling water
1 cup cold water
½ teaspoon salt

2 packages cream cheese
1 cup whipped cream
3 tablespoons pimientos
½ cup crushed pineapple

1. Make Jello according to directions on package.
2. Chill in refrigerator until almost thickened (about 1 - 2 hours).
3. Cream the cheese, add to Jello, add whipped cream, salt, pimientos and pineapple.
4. Return to refrigerator until stiff — unmold and serve.

~~~~~~~~~~~~~~~~~~~~

TROPICAL FRUIT MELANGE

(U. of Fla. Agr. Ext. Service
Circular 162)

1 cup full-ripe seeded Surinam
cherries
1 cup diced pineapple
1 cup orange sections or
grapefruit sections

1 cup papaya balls
½ cup sliced mango
½ cup shredded coconut
½ to 1 cup mango, roselle or
guava syrup

1. Mix all fruit. Cover with syrup. Chill 4 - 6 hours before serving.

FRUIT SALAD (serves 8)

(Mrs. James D. Camp, Jr.)

1 cup green grapes
⅟ package frozen mixed fruit
1 cup diced orange
2 cups miniature marshmallows

1 cup crushed pineapple
1 package frozen raspberries
1 cup diced banana

Dressing:

2 eggs
2 tablespoons vinegar
1 tablespoon butter
2 cups sour cream

2 tablespoons sugar
2 tablespoons orange juice
Dash salt

1. In small pan mix beaten eggs with sugar and orange juice. Add vinegar. Cook stirring constantly until thick. Remove from heat.
2. Stir in butter, salt. Cool.
3. When cool, fold in sour cream.
4. Have all fruit thawed. Combine fruits and marshmallow.
5. Fold dressing into fruit.
6. Place in refrigerator for at least 24 hours.

NOTE: This does not get "hard" like a gelatine salad.

COCONUT FRUIT BOWL (serves 8)

(Mrs. Robert L. Moore)

1 No. 2 can pineapple tidbits
well drained
1 cup seedless grapes
1⅓ cups flaked coconut
¼ teaspoon salt

1 can mandarin orange sections,
(11 ounce can) well drained
1 cup tiny marshmallows
2 cups sour cream

1. Combine fruits and marshmallows. Stir in sour cream and salt.
2. Chill overnight.

OVERNIGHT SALAD (serves 14)

(Mrs. R. C. McGuire)

2 eggs
36 marshmallows
1 cup walnuts or pecans

Juice of 2 lemons
1 large can sliced pineapple
1 pint whipped cream

1. In sauce pan beat eggs and add lemon juice. Boil until thick, stirring constantly.

2. While hot add cut up marshmallows, stirring until completely dissolved. Cool mixture.

3. When mixture is cold add well-drained pineapple and the nut meats which have been cut up. Fold in whipped cream.

4. Refrigerate overnight.

AVOCADO GINGER ALE SALAD

(Mrs. John E. Morris)

2 tablespoons unflavored gelatin
2 cups ginger ale
Juice of 1½ lemons
¼ teaspoon salt

1½ cups diced avocado
1 cup boiling water
¾ cup sugar
4 tablespoons crushed or diced pineapple (canned)

1. Soak gelatine in a little cold water until soft. Add boiling water. Stir to dissolve. Add ginger ale, sugar, lemon juice, salt and pineapple.

2. Pour mold half full of gelatin mixture. When starts to thicken add avocado and balance of gelatine mixture. Refrigerate until firm.

3. Unmold and serve on lettuce with mayonnaise dressing.

GREEN BEAN SALAD

(Mrs. Mary Emma Warriner)

4 cups cooked green beans or
2 cans French style green
  beans
½ cup salad oil
¼ teaspoon Accent

Dash garlic salt
⅓ cup vinegar
3 tablespoons sugar
¾ teaspoon salt
¾ cup chopped onion

1. Mix all ingredients together.
2. Marinate for at least one day in covered container in refrigerator.

~~~~~~~~~~~~~~~~~~~~~~

HOT POTATO SALAD

(Mrs. Chas. F. Schwarm)

4 cups sliced boiled potatoes
1 large onion, chopped fine
6 thick slices bacon, cut into
  small pieces

½ cup vinegar
1 tablespoon salt
½ cup sugar

1. Cook potatoes until done but **not soft.**
2. In pan cook bacon and drain off most of the fat.
3. Add vinegar, salt, dash pepper and cook until blended. If cooks down too much, add 2 tablespoons of water.
4. Add sugar and onions, cook until mixture boils.
5. Put potatoes in pan or casserole. Pour vinegar-bacon mixture over potatoes and let stand at least 3 - 4 hours.
(It is better if you can store in refrigerator 3 - 4 days.)
6. Heat to serve.

NOTE: Short-cut method. Use canned boiled potatoes in place of boiled raw potatoes.

CAESAR-AVOCADO SALAD (serves 6 - 8)

(Mrs. Arch Campbell)

5 heads romaine lettuce
2 cloves garlic
½ cup salad oil
½ teaspoon salt
½ cup lime juice (or lemon)
1 cup croutons (which have been tossed in ¼ cup garlic oil)

½ cup olive oil
2 avocados
3 teaspoons Worcestershire
¾ cup grated Parmesan cheese
1 raw egg

1. Slice garlic cloves into ½ cup olive oil. Let stand at room temperature for at least 2 hours. Remove garlic. Use ¼ cup of this oil to soak the croutons.
2. Cut avocados into slices or cubes and put in bowl. Pull apart the chilled romaine lettuce and add to avocado. Add remaining ¼ cup of olive oil, salad oil, Worcestershire, salt, cheese, egg and lime juice. Toss to coat the greens.
3. Add croutons and serve immediately.

NOTE: 1 pound cooked cleaned shrimp added to this will make a fine luncheon salad. Put in individual bowls and garnish each with shrimp, slices of avocado and sprigs of parsley.

~~~~~~~~~~~~~~~~~~~

KIDNEY BEAN SALAD

(Mrs. Tom G. Lively)

2 large cans kidney beans
1 small onion finely chopped
1 teaspoon dry mustard
2 tablespoons vinegar

2 teaspoons dry horseradish
1 tablespoon Worcestershire
¼ cup chopped celery
Dash salt
Dash pepper

1. Drain beans well. Add all ingredients. Let stand for about 4 hours before serving.
2. **Optional:** Chop one hard boiled egg and mix into salad and slice one egg on top.

NOTE: This is good salad for picnics or boating. No milk or egg products in salad to spoil if salad should get warm.

MOLDED GREEN BEAN SALAD

(Mrs. Oscar P. Pearson)

1 envelope gelatine
½ cup cold bean juice
1 cup boiling water
2 cups cooked green beans
  (or 1 can green beans)

⅓ cup sugar
½ teaspoon salt
4 tablespoons lime juice
1 small can pimiento

1. Make gelatine: Dissolve gelatine powder in cold bean juice. Add sugar, salt and boiling water and stir until dissolved.

2. Add lime juice, cut green beans and cut pimientoes.

3. Pour into mold and chill 3 - 4 hours in refrigerator.

SHORT-CUT: Use package jello either lemon or lime flavor. Make according to instructions on box using cold bean juice in place of some of the water.

~~~~~~~~~~~~~~~~~~~~~~

VEGETABLE SALAD (serves 8)

(Recipe Selection Committee)

1 package frozen peas
1 package frozen wax beans
¼ cup sour cream
1 teaspoon dry mustard
¼ cup finely chopped onion
1 package frozen lima beans

½ cup French Dressing
¼ cup mayonnaise
Dash salt
Dash pepper
¼ cup finely chopped celery

1. Cook all vegetables as directed on packages. Drain and plunge into cold water. Let stand 5 minutes. Drain. Put into bowl, add French Dressing, stir, cover and refrigerate for 2 - 4 hours. Toss several times.

2. Drain vegetables. Mix mayonnaise, sour cream, mustard, salt, pepper. Put dressing on vegetables, add celery and onion. Toss and serve.

ZIPPY GREEN SALAD

(Mrs. Arch Campbell)

Dressing:

½ cup olive oil
Dash white peper
1 clove garlic chopped fine

⅓ cup lemon juice
Dash salt

1. Beat with rotary beater and chill in refrigerator at least one hour before using.

Salad:

Break into bowl: One head lettuce, one head bib lettuce, 1 bunch watercress, ½ cup green cabbage, ½ cup red cabbage.

Pour dressing over greens. Top bowl with slices of chilled beets.

~~~~~~~~~~~~~~~~

SPINACH SALAD

(Mrs. Tom G. Lively)

1 pound fresh spinach
2 hard cooked eggs
¼ cup crisp crumbled bacon

¼ cup salad oil
¼ cup wine

1. Wash spinach, dry. Tear into bits in large bowl.
2. Mix oil, wine, bacon chips. Chop egg fine. Add to oil mix. Let stand about 1 hour.
3. Pour oil mix over spinach. Serve at once.

~~~~~~~~~~~~~~~~

SLAW DRESSING

(Recipe Selection Committee)

2 tablespoons sugar
1 teaspoon dry mustard

½ cup vinegar
Salt
Pepper

1. Add dry mustard to vinegar, stir. Add sugar, salt and pepper.
2. Let stand for about one hour, then pour over thinly sliced cabbage.

NOTE: For variation: In pan dice two strips bacon and fry until crisp. Add Slaw Dressing and bring to boil. Pour immediately over cabbage.

CRANBERRY CREAM SALAD (serves 4 - 6)

(Mrs. Max H. Chapman)

1 package cherry Jello
1 can whole cranberry sauce
¼ cup chopped nuts

¼ cup hot water
½ cup diced celery
1 cup sour cream

1. Dissolve Jello in hot water. Stir in cranberry sauce, nuts, celery and sour cream.
2. Pour into dish and refrigerate until firm.

NEVER FAIL HOLLANDAISE SAUCE

(Mrs. Spencer S. Thomas)

2 egg yolks
½ cup melted butter
Speck cayenne pepper

½ teaspoon salt
1 tablespoon lemon juice

1. Beat yolks until thick. Add salt, pepper. Mix.
2. Add one tablespoon melted butter at a time stirring or beating constantly. Beat butter and lemon juice alternately.

NOTE: Can be made ahead of time. If so, refrigerate. To serve, stir over lukewarm water (never hot) until softened.

LIME SALAD DRESSING

(Mrs. Mary Tsolas)

4 tablespoons lime juice
¼ cup Florida orange juice
½ teaspoon salt
Dash paprika
2 tablespoons vinegar

2 tablespoons sugar
¾ cup salad oil
Optional: 4 tablespoons chopped fresh mint

1. Combine all ingredients in covered jar. Shake to blend.
2. Refrigerate. Flavor improves with age.

LIME-YOGHURT FRUIT DRESSING

(Mrs. Tom G. Lively)

8 ounces plain yoghurt

½ teaspoon salt

2 teaspoons lime rind, grated

¼ cup honey

½ teaspoon dry mustard

4 teaspoons Key lime juice

1. Add mustard to lime juice and let stand for a minute.
2. Beat with fork - yoghurt, honey, salt. Add lime juice and rind. Mix thoroughly.

NOTE: Wonderful light dressing for fresh fruit salads - easy on the calories also.

~~~~~~~~~~~~

HEAD LETTUCE DRESSING

(1924 Woman's Club Cook Book)

1 cake Philadelphia cream cheese

Juice of half lime (or lemon)

½ teaspoon sugar

3 tablespoons catsup or chili sauce

½ teaspoon paprika

4 tablespoons olive oil

4 tablespoons vinegar

1 diced green pepper

2 hard boiled eggs

1. Mix cheese, olive oil. Add lime juice and vinegar.
2. Mash eggs with fork. Mix into cheese mixture.
3. Add sugar, catsup, pepper, paprika. Mix well.
4. If dressing tastes oily, add a little more vinegar.

FRENCH DRESSING

(Mrs. Wm. G. Crawford)

1 medium sized onion, grated
4 tablespoons vinegar
¼ teaspoon black pepper
1 cup salad oil

3 tablespoons sugar
1 teaspoon salt
2 tablespoons catsup

1. Mix all ingredients in jar. Shake well. Store in covered jar in refrigerator.

FRENCH DRESSING (no sugar)

(Mrs. Eugene D. Koch)

1 cup oil
2 tablespoons water
1 tablespoon salt

⅓ cup cider vinegar
1 garlic clove
¼ teaspoon paprika

1. Mash garlic clove with salt and paprika.
2. Into bottle pour oil, water, vinegar and add mashed garlic.
3. Shake well. Let stand short time before using.

LIME SOUR CREAM DRESSING

(Mrs. Wm. E. Lemkau)

2 teaspoons lime juice
2 tablespoons confectioners sugar

½ cup sour cream

1. Mix lime juice, sugar and sour cream.

NOTE: To be used on fruit salads, gelatine desserts.

HONEY FRUIT DRESSING

(Mrs. Ben A. Bollinger)

¼ cup honey
½ pint whipping cream

1 cup mayonnaise

1. Whip cream. Mix honey with mayonnaise. Fold whipped cream into mayonnaise mixture.

HONEY-ORANGE DRESSING

(Mrs. Wm. E. Lemkau)

2 tablespoons honey
2 tablespoons orange juice

1 cup sour cream

1. Blend honey and orange juice then fold in sour cream.

NOTE: Use on fruit salads or on gelatine desserts.

FRUIT DRESSING

(Mrs. Ben A. Bollinger)

¾ cup confectioners sugar
1 teaspoon salt
Dash paprika
1 teaspoon onion juice
1 cup oil

1 teaspoon dry mustard
3 tablespoons vinegar
1 teaspoon celery seed
1 tablespoon lemon juice

1. Mix sugar, mustard, salt, vinegar and paprika in a bowl. Let stand for 3 - 4 hours. Stir occasionally.

2. Add celery seed, onion juice, lemon juice and oil. Beat until consistency of honey (blender can be used).

OLD CITY DOCKS, FORT LAUDERDALE, FLORIDA

Seafood and Fish

I never lost a little fish - yes, I am free to say
It was always the biggest fish I caught that got away.

Our Biggest Fish
Eugene Field
(1850-1895)

WHICH IS BEST

What is the best eating fish taken in Florida waters?

The gourmets have never settled it among themselves, most standing firm for pompano, but a resolute minority declare unequivocably that the yellowtail is far superior.

The common run of fish eater is likely to disagree with both schools of thought. There is many a solid trencherman who holds for the dolphin as superior to all others, and there are even many who declare that only a matter of its unprepossessing exterior appearance prevents the lowly blowfish from occupying the top spot.

One of the principal assets of the pompano is the fact that it can be preserved and shipped so easily without loss of either texture or flavor. Another strong point is that it lends itself to any kind of cooking. You can bake it, broil it, fry it, or even boil it, and it is good! The buttery flesh also lends itself readily to garnishment with such exotic flourishments as ground almonds and tropical fruits.

Often taken by anglers off the coast along Southeast Florida is the blackfin tuna, a smaller cousin of the giant bluefin. This fish is usually discarded by anglers as unworthy of the skillet. Actually it can provide a gastronomical treat second to none. These fish average five to twenty pounds. They should be filleted and the skin removed, then boiled. It will be found to be infinitely superior in taste and texture to any kind of canned tuna fish.

The bonita and Arctic bonita are also frequently caught and discarded. They can be treated in the same fashion to make a delicious family treat. Cooked in the ordinary fashion these fish are good but dark in appearance because of the great amount of blood which is easily boiled off. If a dark streak shows down the side of the cooked fish it can be easily lifted out.

The yellowtail should be broiled or fried. The dolphin can be cooked in a variety of ways but is best fried. Both the blowfish and the grunt are strictly frying size.

Those of us who suffered through the long depression will never outlive our gratitude to the despised grunt. Admittedly the most attractive thing about the grunt was its absolute willingness to be caught with a minimum of effort and expense and at any time or tide. The era of "grits and grunts" was a trying period in Fort Lauderdale's history, but one which many now refer to with real pride. The sweet, if bony, meat is still a mouth-watering memory.

Years ago, when Okeechobee catfish were a delicacy and were being relished throughout the nation, the banks of New River were lined with tin fish houses, and I was a kid of nine. I caught my first fish of importance, a 17-pound river cat. It was a proud moment when I walked across the old Andrews Avenue Bridge with a hand under each gill, holding the fish chin high so its tail wouldn't drag, and it was rendered prouder by the fact that I met my mother and two other very "dressed-up" ladies crossing the bridge from the other direction.

Admittedy my clothes were a bit messy and disheveled, but I **never** understood why "Ma" didn't share my pride. It didn't discourage me. I promptly sold the cat to a fish house for a munificent 34 cents.

I have been fishing ever since, and cooking them, and cleaning them, and eating them. Which is the best? To me a blue runner **boiled** in a tin can full of salt water when I have found shelter on a **rainy** day tastes best.

—Philip Weidling

~~~~~~~~~~~~~~~~~~~~~~~~~~~

SEAFOOD AND FISHES

The following list is a guide which will help you use some of the many locally found fish.

BLUEFISH — under 4 pounds use as pan fish. Over 4 pounds, fillet.

BLACKFIN TUNA — fillet then boil.

BONITO — fillet then boil.

BRIM — use as pan fish.

CATFISH — this is **fresh water** catfish. Not all catfish found around here is good eating. Use as pan fish.

COBIA — fillet.

CONCH — use in many ways. Can be taken from shell two ways. (1) Saw off tip of shell below third swirl. Use pliers to grab foot and with a twisting motion, pull out of shell. (2) Drop into pan of cold water and bring to boil. Boil for 5 minutes. Remove from water. With pliers, grab foot and with twisting motion, pull out of shell. Cut off foot and eye feelers. Pare skin off.

CRAB — dropped into boiling water. Shell cracked off after cooking.

CRAWFISH — can be cooked whole by dropping into boiling water. Can be split down middle and broiled. Cooked in many ways. Shell taken off after cooking.

DOLPHIN — fillet.

FLOUNDER— under 4 pounds use as pan fish. Over 4 pounds, fillet.

FROGS — use many ways, fried, broiled.

GRUNT — use as pan fish.

GROUPER — fillet.

HOGFISH — use as pan fish.

JEWFISH — fillet

KING — cut into steaks (some people fillet also).

LOOK-DOWN — use as pan fish.

MACKEREL — fillet

MULLET — this is **fresh water** mullet. Not all mullet around here is good eating. Use as pan fish.

PERMIT — fillet.

POMPANO — use as pan fish. Also baked, broiled whole including head, but with insides removed and fins cut off.

SAND PERCH — use as pan fish.

SHRIMP — cook with or without shells. Cook also with or without head. Most people snap off heads, use tail only in cooking.

SNAPPER — fillet.

SNOOK — fillet.

TRIPLETAIL — fillet.

WAHOO — fillet.

YELLOWTAIL — under 4 pounds use as pan fish. Over 4 pounds, fillet.

Note: Clams, oysters and scallops are not generally taken from Broward County waters for eating.

Florida Blue Crab may be substituted for shellfish listed in following recipes:

> Crab Imperial
>
> Chafing Dish Crabmeat
>
> Quick Curried Alaska Crab
>
> Seafood Casserole
>
> Surprise Casserole

Bluefish, Cobia, Dolphin, Flounder, Grouper, Jewfish, Kingfish, Mackerel, Permit, Pompano, Snapper, Snook, Tripletail, Wahoo or Yellowtail may be substituted for any of the fish in the following recipes:

> Broiled Kingfish Steak with Dill
>
> Cioppino Florida Style
>
> Dolphin Flambeau
>
> Fish Gumbo
>
> Fried Fillet
>
> Lime Baked Fish
>
> Mayonnaise Fillet
>
> Sashimi

Bluefish, Brim, Catfish, Flounder, Grunt, Hogfish, Look-Down, Mullet, Pompano, Sand Perch and Yellowtail may be used as Fried Pan Fish.

BOILED CRAWFISH OR BLUE CRAB

(Recipe Selection Committee)

1. Use large kettle. Bring salted, spiced water to boil.
   - (a) Commercial crab-boil may be used.
   - (b) If you are at the ocean, a bucket of fresh clear ocean water may be used.
   - (c) If mixing your own spices use: 1 tablespoon salt, 1 cup white vinegar (or ¼ cup lime juice), 1 tablespoon peppercorns, 1 tablespoon cloves, 2 sticks cinnamon, 1 tablespoon celery seed, 1 tablespoon mustard seed.
2. Drop crawfish or crab into boiling water. Cook for 10 - 15 minutes. Do not overcook.
3. Remove from water, rinse and remove from shell.

For crawfish: Use scissors to cut under shell up the middle. Use knife to cut through meat and back shell. Pull meat out of shell. Remove back vein.

For crab: Remove claws. Discard feeler claws and save large claws. Separate back shell from under-shell by pulling apart. Back shell may be washed and used for serving dishes, to cook in. Discard stomach and spongy piece. Pick meat. Claws may be served whole or may be cracked with hammer or seafood cracker.

QUICK CURRIED ALASKA CRAB (serves 6)

(Mrs. Dwight L. Rogers, Sr.)

1 package frozen patty shells
1 package dry curry mix
Milk
¼ cup toasted almonds, slivered

1 can (4 ounce) mushrooms, drained
2 packages frozen King crab (6 ounce each)

1. Bake patty shells according to directions on package.
2. Prepare curry mix using milk. Add drained mushrooms. Add crab meat which has been thawed. Add almonds.
3. When ready to serve, pour crab mixture over patty shells.

NOTE: You may substitute cooked shrimp.

CRAB IMPERIAL
(Mrs. John W. DeGroot)

2 teaspoons dry mustard
½ teaspoon pepper
2 tablespoons Worcestershire
2 raw eggs
5 to 6 large crackers (Sea Toast type)
2 tablespoons sherry

½ teaspoon salt
2 or 3 dashes Tabasco
1 tablespoon capers
4 tablespoons mayonnaise
1 pound crab meat, cooked
3 or 4 slices mild cheese, cut up

1. In large bowl mix mustard, salt, pepper, Tabasco, Worcestershire, capers, eggs, mayonnaise, sherry. Mix well. Add cheese pieces. Crush the crackers, add.

2. Check crab meat for bits of shell. Leave in good-sized pieces. Gently toss crab in seasoned mixture.

3. Pile gently into two large scallop shells.

4. Heat in 500° oven until golden. Serve immediately.

CHAFING DISH CRAB MEAT (serves 3)
(Mrs. Dwight L. Rogers, Jr.)

1 pound crab meat, lump style
4 tablespoons tarragon vinegar (or 2 sprigs fresh tarragon leaves, or 1 tablespoon dry tarragon)
Fresh ground pepper and salt to taste

½ cup butter
2 tablespoons Worcestershire sauce
½ cup chopped chives
½ cup chopped parsley

1. Check crab meat for shells. Heat in double boiler until just warm. Add vinegar, Worcestershire, salt, pepper, chives, tarragon and parsley.

2. In chafing dish heat butter until very hot but not brown. Toss in crab meat mixture.

JAMBALAYA SHRIMP (serves 6)

(Mrs. Tom M. Bryan)

1 tablespoon fat
1 tablespoon flour
1½ cups cooked tomatoes
1 clove garlic, crushed
1 tablespoon minced parsley
1 teaspoon Worcestershire
  sauce
4 cups water
1 pound cooked ham, chopped

1½ cups cooked shrimp
1 onion, sliced
1 green pepper, chopped
1 red pepper, chopped
1 cup uncooked rice
Dash salt
Dash pepper
Dash paprika

1. Melt fat. Add flour, stirring until slightly brown and smooth.
2. Add ham, shrimp, tomatoes and cook for about 3 minutes.
3. Add rice, water, garlic, parsley, Worcestershire, onion, and pepper. Cover pot and boil until tender, or about 30 minutes. Do not stir. It may be necessary to scrape bottom of kettle from time to time to keep rice from burning.

CREOLE SHRIMP (serves 4)

(Mrs. Terry Tower)

1 pound cooked shrimp
1 medium onion, chopped
1 green pepper, diced
½ cup chopped fresh
  mushrooms
1 teaspoon chili powder
Salt and pepper to taste

¼ cup bacon drippings
2 tablespoons flour
1 can condensed tomato soup
2 cups fresh tomatoes
1 tablespoon minced parsley
Steamed or boiled rice

1. Melt fat in skillet. Cook onion and green pepper until soft. Add mushrooms. Sprinkle in flour and mix well.
2. Dilute soup with half the amount of water called for on the can. Add soup to onion-pepper mix. Add tomatoes, shrimp, chili powder, parsley, salt and pepper. Simmer 10 minutes.
3. Serve over rice.

SHRIMP AND RICE (serves 4)

(Mrs. Louie Hamilton)

1½ pounds fresh shrimp
1 small package yellow rice
½ stick butter

1 bag shrimp boil (or use your
own favorite spices)
3 cups water

1. Wash and peel shrimp. Split down back and remove vein. Rinse.
2. In large pot put 3 cups water and some salt and bring to boil. Add shrimp boil bag (or your spices) and the shrimp.
3. Boil the shrimp for 3 minutes if small, 5 minutes if large.
4. Remove shrimp and boil bag from water. Put rice into water. Cook until rice is tender (about 15 minutes) adding a little water if necessary.
5. Put shrimp with rice, add butter and serve hot.

NOTE: With green salad and garlic bread this is a complete meal.

SHERRY SHRIMP AND RICE (serves 12)

(Mrs. Max H. Chapman)

2 cans frozen shrimp soup
1 package (3 ounce) garlic
flavored cheese
⅛ teaspoon pepper
2 packages frozen cooked
shrimp (or 2 pounds)
Hot rice

½ cup coffee cream
1 can (4 ounce) mushrooms
½ teaspoon Accent
½ teaspoon salt
1 package frozen peas, cooked
½ cup sherry

1. Blend soup, cheese, cream in heavy saucepan over low heat. When hot, add seasonings, peas, mushrooms and shrimp.
2. Heat to simmering. Pour into chafing dish on mounds of hot parslied rice.

CHAFING DISH SHRIMP

(Mrs. Nelson B. Thomas)

2 cans undiluted tomato soup
3 small packages cream cheese
¼ cup diced onion
3 cups cooked shrimp

½ cup diced green pepper
¾ cup diced celery
½ teaspoon salt
1 cup mayonnaise

1. Heat soup in top of double boiler. Add cheese and stir occasionally until cheese has melted.

2. Add onion, pepper, celery, salt, shrimp and mayonnaise. Stir well and heat only until shrimp are hot. **Do not boil.**

3. Transfer to chafing dish and serve.

NOTE: May be made a day in advance and kept in refrigerator. Just heat to serve. May be used on rice, toast, biscuits.

SURPRISE CASSEROLE (serves 4)

(Mrs. Phoebe N. Conklin)

1 medium sized cabbage
1 can peas
1½ pounds raw or cooked
   shrimp

1 can mushroom soup
2 medium potatoes, cooked and
   mashed
2 tablespoons butter

1. Parboil cabbage, quarter and remove hard heart.

2. Line casserole dish with broken cabbage.

3. Empty peas, shrimp and soup into center of dish. Add dash salt, pepper. Put butter in bits over top.

4. Cover top with mashed potato.

5. Bake at 350° for about 20 minutes or until potatoes are lightly browned and it is heated through.

NOTE: Crab or lobster may be used in place of shrimp or in combination with shrimp.

CRAB PATTIES

(Mrs. John W. DeGroot)

2 teaspoons dry mustard
½ teaspoon pepper
2 tablespoons Worcestershire
2 raw eggs
1 pound cooked crab meat
6 large Sea Toast crackers

½ teaspoon salt
3 dashes Tabasco
1 tablespoon capers
4 tablespoons mayonnaise
Cracker crumbs

1. Crush the Sea Toast crackers to make fine crumbs. Put in large bowl. Add mustard, salt, pepper, Tabasco, Worcestershire, capers, mayonnaise and raw egg. Mix well.
2. Check cooked crab for shell bits. Leave in good-sized pieces. Fold crab into seasoned crumb mixture. Spread on large flat platter and refrigerate for 2 - 3 hours.
3. When ready to use, remove from refrigerator, shape into patties, and press into cracker crumbs.
4. Fry in hot oil until golden brown. Serve at once.

CRAWFISH THERMIDOR (serves 4)

(Mrs. Tom G. Lively)

4 boiled crawfish tails
4 tablespoons butter
4 tablespoons flour
1 cup cream
½ cup grated cheese
1 tablespoon chopped chives

½ teaspoon mustard
4 tablespoons sherry
1 egg yolk
¼ teaspoon salt
1 cup fresh sliced mushrooms
Dash paprika

1. Make white sauce: Melt butter in pan, stir in flour, add cream, salt, mustard, egg yolks, mushrooms, chives. Heat until thick. If hard to stir, add a little water. Remove from heat, add sherry.
2. Remove meat from split tails. Cut meat into chunks and add to white sauce.
3. Wash and clean shells. Sprinkle little cheese in shell, heap lobster mixture and sprinkle cheese on top with dash paprika.
4. Bake at 375° until brown (about 20 minutes).

CRAWFISH NEWBURG (serves 4)

(Mrs. Tom G. Lively)

2 cups cooked crawfish
2 tablespoons lime juice
2 egg yolks
Dash salt
Dash pepper

3 tablespoons butter
¾ cup evaporated milk
¼ cup sherry

1. Cut crawfish into bite sizes and sprinkle with lime juice. Let stand 5 minutes.
2. Melt butter in pan, add crawfish.
3. Beat egg yolks, add cream to yolks, mix well.
4. Stirring constantly, add cream mixture to crawfish. Leave on fire until slightly thick. Remove from heat, add salt, pepper. Add sherry.
5. To serve, pour on toast triangles, or over rice.

CIOPPINO FLORIDA STYLE (serves 8 - 10)

(Recipe Selection Committee)

¼ cup olive oil
1 cup chopped onion
1 large can tomatoes
1 bay leaf, crumbled
1 pound crawfish tails
1 pound cleaned shrimp
1 teaspoon salt
2 cups dry white wine

2 minced garlic cloves
1 cup chopped green pepper
1 can tomato sauce (8 ounce)
¼ teaspoon oregano
1 pound flounder fillet
1 can minced clams
½ teaspoon pepper

1. Heat oil in large heavy pan. Add garlic, onion, green pepper and cook until lightly brown (about 10 minutes). Add tomatoes, tomato sauce, bay leaf, oregano, salt, pepper. If using raw crawfish, shrimp and fillet, cut these into small pieces and add now (if using all cooked seafood add in step 2). Cover pan and simmer for about 1 hour. Stir often.
2. Add clams and wine. (If using cooked crawfish, shrimp and fillet, add now.) Simmer for 10 minutes.

NOTE: Serve with hot French bread. This is a complete meal.

QUICK OYSTER CASSEROLE (serves 4)

(Mrs. Jay Forbes)

1 pint oysters
2 tablespoons chopped celery tops
2 tablespoons butter
¼ teaspoon salt
2 cups cracker crumbs

1 can condensed mushroom soup
1 teaspoon minced onion
¼ cup milk or cream
Butter to grease dish

1. Grease casserole dish with butter. Put in oysters, soup, onion, celery greens and 1½ cups of the crumbs. Mix well.

2. Pour milk over top. Break butter into bits and put on top of oyster mixture. Sprinkle remaining crumbs over top.

3. Bake for 30 minutes at 350°.

SCALLOPS STROGANOFF (serves 6)

(Mrs. Tom G. Lively)

2 pounds scallops
1 bay leaf
2 whole cloves
1 tablespoon salad oil
1 can tomato sauce (8 ounce)
⅛ teaspoon oregano
3 cups boiling water

1 slice lime
2 tablespoons minced onion
1 tablespoon minced parsley
1 cup sour cream
⅛ teaspoon marjoram
Salt
Pepper

1. In kettle place scallops and boiling water to cover. Add bay leaf, cloves, and lime slice. Simmer 10 minutes.

2. In fry pan, heat oil and add onions. Cook lightly. Add tomato sauce, parsley, oregano, marjoram, salt, pepper and sour cream. Remove from heat.

3. In greased casserole arrange well-drained scallops. Pour sauce over scallops.

4. Put under broiler, about 4 inches from flame and heat about 3 - 4 minutes or until lightly brown. Serve at once.

SEA FOOD CASSEROLE (serves 10 - 12)

(Mrs. Eugene D. Koch)

3 cups cooked rice
½ green pepper, chopped
2 tablespoons butter
2 pounds cooked cleaned shrimp
1 can frozen undiluted creamed shrimp soup

Buttered bread crumbs
1 small onion chopped
1 can tomatoes
1 can condensed mushroom soup
1 pound cleaned cooked crab
3 tablespoons sherry
Grated Parmesan cheese

1. Melt butter in pan. Brown onion and green pepper.

2. Add tomatoes and cook about 5 minutes. Add rice.

3. Grease utility dish (about 8 x 11 inches). Pour tomato mixture into pan, pour in mushroom soup mixture.

4. Mix shrimp, crab, and shrimp soup. Add sherry. Pour over rice mixture. Sprinkle crumbs and cheese on top.

5. Bake one hour at 325°.

ESCALLOPED KINGFISH

(1924 Woman's Club Cook Book)

2 cups cooked fish
2 tablespoons butter
1 sprig parsley
Dash cayenne
¼ teaspoon pepper

1 pint milk
2 tablespoons flour
¼ onion
1 teaspoon salt
½ cup bread crumbs, buttered

1. Use cooked fish which has no skin and no bones left in.

2. Make white sauce: Melt butter in pan, add flour, milk and cook until thickened. Add cayenne, pepper, onion, salt.

3. Butter baking dish. Put in layer of fish, then layer of white sauce.

4. Top with buttered bread crumbs.

5. Bake in oven approximately 30 minutes at 350° or until top is browned. Sprinkle parsley over top and serve.

LIME BAKED FISH (serves 4)

(Mrs. Arch Campbell)

2 pounds fresh fish fillets
1 teaspoon grated lime rind
½ teaspoon salt
1 tablespoon Worcestershire

½ cup lime juice
1½ tablespoons finely chopped onion
⅛ teaspoon pepper

1. Place fish in shallow pan.
2. Mix lime juice, rind, salt, pepper, Worcestershire and onion. Pour over fish. Let stand at room temperature for about 1 hour.
3. Bake for 20 - 25 minutes at 350° or until fish flakes.
4. Pour pan juice over fish and serve.

FRIED PAN FISH

(Recipe Selection Committtee)

1 egg
Cleaned pan fish

1 cup cracker crumbs (or cornmeal)

1. Have pan fish cleaned. Cut off head and tail. With scissors cut off fins. Wash fish and dry.
2. Dip fish into beaten egg, then into crumbs.
3. Have pan with hot oil (not butter as it will burn) about ½ inch deep in pan. Drop fish into hot oil (**Do not** put fish into cool oil).
4. Brown well, turn and brown on other side. Serve at once.

MAYONNAISE FILLET

(Recipe Selection Committee)

1 fillet per person

2 tablespoons mayonnaise per fillet

1. Arrange fillet on broiler rack. Spread one tablespoon mayonnaise on each. Broil about 4 inches from flame for 5 minutes. Turn. Spread one tablespoon mayonnaise on other side and broil for 5 minutes (or until meat flaky).
2. Serve at once with lime or lemon slices.

DOLPHIN FLAMBEAU (serves 4)

(Robert Youngblood)

4 dolphin fillets	½ small bottle orange extract
4 tablespoons butter	(must have 70 to 80%
¼ pound slivered almonds	alcohol)

1. Melt butter in pan. Put dolphin on broiler rack and brush with some of the butter.
2. Broil dolphin about 3 inches from flame for about 5 minutes. Turn. Brush other side with butter and broil about 5 minutes. Meat should be white and flaky but not browned. Remove from broiler pan and arrange on serving dish.
3. Brown almonds in remaining butter in pan. Spread browned almonds over fillets.
4. Pour orange extract over dolphin, light and serve at once.

NOTE: Great dish for those special dinners.

BROILED CATFISH

(Mrs. Robert S. Pendleton)

2 pounds catfish	Parsley
¼ pound butter	2 teaspoons salt
¼ teaspoon pepper	2 tablespoons flour

1. Skin catfish. (Put fish on back. Take knife and cut almost through to back. Cut around head, turn head back and pull head and skin off at same time.)
2. Cut fish in half. Wash and wipe dry.
3. Mix flour, salt, pepper. Roll fish in mixture.
4. Melt butter, add parsley.
5. Place catfish on broiler pan. Brush butter mixture on fish. Broil for 5 minutes on each side. Brush with rest of butter.
6. Serve at once with slice of lime or lemon.

POMPANO ALMONDINE

(Recipe Selection Committee)

1 Pompano per person Butter
Slivered almonds Greased paper

1. Have insides removed from Pompano. With scissors trim tail and fins. Wash and pat dry (fish is cooked with head).

2. Grease heavy paper with butter or oil. Lay Pompano in single layer on greased paper. (You may wrap fish separately or several together.) Overlap the paper and secure lap with toothpicks or skewer.

3. Lay in shallow pan. Place pan in oven for 30 minutes at 350°.

4. In saucepan melt butter. Put almonds in butter and brown.

5. Remove fish from paper carefully so as not to tear skin. Lay on platter and pour buttered almonds over fish.

NOTE: For special occasions use parchment-type paper.

ALTERNATE METHOD: Put two tablespoons butter and two tablespoons slivered almonds over each fish before pinning paper. Serve at table unopened. Let each diner open his own.

SASHIMI (raw fish)

(Recipe Selection Committee)

Select a sea fish fillet which is firm and fresh.
Cut fillet into bite-sized pieces. Serve ice cold in serving dish with a dipping sauce.

For Sashimi: Dolphin, Snapper, King and Shrimp.

Dipping Sauce: Equal parts of lime juice and soy sauce. Mix well and chill.

BROILED KINGFISH STEAKS WITH DILL (serves 4)

(Mrs. Alvin Ray)

4 kingfish steaks ½ to ¾ inch thick

4 tablespoons butter, melted

½ tablespoon lime (or lemon juice)

Dash dried or fresh dill

1. Make lemon butter by mixing melted butter and lime juice.

2. Arrange kingfish steaks on broiler pan. Brush steaks with lemon butter. Sprinkle a little dill on top of each.

3. Put steaks 3 inches from flame and cook about 5 minutes.

4. Turn steaks, brush with lemon butter and sprinkle dill on top of each. Return to broiler and broil another 5 minutes, or until fish is lightly brown.

BAKED STUFFED KINGFISH (serves 6)

(Recipe Selection Committee)

1 kingfish which has had insides removed, head, tail and fins cut off

2 cups bread stuffing

3 slices bacon

Butter

Salt

Pepper

1. Wash fish and dry. Sprinkle cavity with salt and pepper. Stuff lightly with dressing. Skewer or sew cavity. Place fish on greased pan.

2. Bake fish for 40 - 60 minutes at 350 or until fish is tender. Fish may dry out so baste with oil or butter. Some like to lay strips of bacon on top of fish.

3. To serve: Place fish on platter, surround with parsley, lime or lemon slices, or bits of citrus fruit.

BROILED FROG'S LEGS

(Mrs. Robert S. Pendleton)

Frog's legs
½ cup butter

Salt, pepper, parsley, dill
Lemon juice (or lime juice)

1. Place frog's legs on broiler pan.
2. Melt butter. Add salt, pepper, parsley, dill and lime juice.
3. Brush legs with butter mix.
4. Place under pre-heated broiler flame, about 3 inches from flame. Broil 5 minutes, brushing with butter mix several times.
5. Turn over, brush with butter mix and broil for 5 more minutes, brushing several times with butter mix.
6. Serve at once with slice of lime (or lemon).

FRIED FROG'S LEGS (serves 4)

(Recipe Selection Committee)

12 jumbo legs (or 24 small legs)
Flour with salt, pepper

Egg batter and crumbs
Oil and butter

1. Wash legs well. Dip into beaten egg and then into bread or cracker or cornmeal crumbs.
2. Have about ½ inch oil in bottom of fry pan. When hot put in legs. Brown on one side. Turn, put pat of butter into oil and brown. Drain on paper towel and serve at once.

TUNA SUBSTITUTE

(Mrs. Robert S. Pendleton)

1. Boil kingfish until white and flaky.
2. Use favorite tuna recipe but substitute the boiled kingfish for the tuna.

TUNA FISH (fresh)

(Philip Weidling)

1. Fillet and skin the fish.
2. Put in water and bring to rolling boil. Boil for 5 minutes. Pour off water. Put fresh water on fish, bring to rolling boil again for 5 minutes, pour off water. Do this a total of 3 times.

NOTE: Resulting fish is white, firm but flaky. Same instructions may be used for bonito.

ALMOND TUNA LOAF (serves 8)

(Mrs. Tom G. Lively)

1½ cups cooked macaroni
½ cup chopped onion
1 teaspoon salt
½ cup water
½ cup sliced roasted almonds
2 cans tuna fish (6½ ounce each or 2 cups fresh cooked tuna)
1 tablespoon lime juice

½ cup butter
½ cup flour
2 cans evaporated milk (13 ounce)
3 eggs
Dash salt
2 tablespoons pimiento
½ teaspoon dill weed

1. Melt butter in saucepan. Add onion and saute lightly. Stir in flour and salt, add milk and water, stirring until smooth and thick. Stir in almonds. Remove from heat.
2. Beat eggs slightly. Measure 2 cups of white sauce and mix in with eggs. Add macaroni and well-drained tuna fish.
3. Line pan with foil (9x5x3 inch pan). Put tuna mix in pan.
4. Bake for 40 minutes at 375°. Remove from oven and cool for 5 minutes. Lift out of pan and place tuna loaf on platter.
5. Re-heat remaining sauce, stir in cut up pimientos, lime juice, and dill weed.
6. Pour sauce over top of loaf. Serve loaf sliced with sauce on each piece.

FISH GUMBO (serves 4)

(Mrs. Tom G. Lively)

1 chopped onion	1 chopped green pepper
¼ cup butter	1 can tomatoes (19 ounce)
1 teaspoon salt	½ teaspoon celery salt
1 bay leaf	½ teaspoon thyme
1 diced red pepper	2 cups raw okra
1 pound mackerel fillet cut in small pieces	Hot rice for 4

1. Melt butter in pan. Add onion and pepper and cook for 5 minutes. Add salt, bay leaf, pepper, tomatoes, celery salt, thyme. Cook for 10 minutes.

2. Add okra, cook 10 more minutes; add fish and cook 10 more minutes.

3. Serve over rice.

FRIED FISH FILLET

(Recipe Selection Committee)

1 fish fillet per person	Egg, slightly beaten
Flour with salt, pepper	Cooking oil

1. Cut fillet into serving size pieces. Wash and dry. Dip into egg then into seasoned flour.

2. Pour cooking oil into fry pan at least ½ inch deep. Heat to smoking stage.

3. Drop floured fish into hot fat. Brown on both sides.

NOTE: Corn meal may be used instead of flour.

OLD SOUR

(Mrs. Alfred J. Beck)

Juice of limes to make 1½ pints juice (approx.)

1 tablespoon salt
4-5 red peppers (bird or cayenne)

1. Put juice in bottle, add salt and drop peppers in whole.
2. Set in sun for two days.
3. When using, don't worry about the "Mother" - just shake well.

NOTE: This is an old Key West recipe for use on fish. This may be kept for years. Do use with caution as this is a highly concentrated flavoring.

SPANISH SAUCE FOR FISH

(Mrs. John H. Fidler,
1917 So. Methodist Cook Book)

3 onions, chopped fine
1 small can tomatoes
½ pint cooked peas
¼ teaspoon salt

1 tablespoon cooking oil
1 small chopped pepper (green)
Dash red pepper
Optional: ¼ cup chopped olives

1. Cook onion and green pepper until soft in cooking oil. Add tomatoes, olives, peas, red pepper and salt. Heat and serve.

NOTE: Use this sauce to bake fish. Also put on top of fried or broiled fish when ready to serve.

FISH SAUCE

(Mrs. Magnus Loftstedt)

½ cup butter
½ cup boiling water
Juice of ½ lemon

2 egg yolks
⅛ teaspoon salt
Dash pepper

1. Cream butter well. Add egg yolks one at time, mix well. Beat in lemon juice, salt and pepper.
2. Place in double boiler and cook until thick.
3. When ready to serve beat in boiling water.

CARIBBEAN PINE, FORT LAUDERDALE, FLORIDA

Soups, Chowders and Stews

Soup of the evening, beautiful soup!

Alice's Adventures in Wonderland
Lewis Carroll
(1832-1898)

CONCH CHOWDER

(Terry Tower)

4 large conchs

¼ pound salt pork

1 large onion

2 quarts water

4 raw potatoes, diced

1 small can tomatoes

1 green pepper

1. Grind conchs.
2. Fry out salt pork in large pan. Add onion, pepper, tomatoes, conchs, potatoes and water.
3. Cook until potatoes fall apart and thicken the chowder (about 1 hour).
4. Turn off heat and let chowder stand several hours.
5. To serve, just re-heat.

NOTE: This chowder has much better flavor if allowed to stand overnight.

~~~~~~~~~~~~~~~~~~~~

QUICK CONCH CHOWDER (serves 8)

(Mrs. Robert Youngblood)

4 cans Manhattan clam chowder   4 conchs

(your favorite brand)

1. Beat conch meat about 10 minutes to tenderize. Using very sharp knife dice conch into about ⅛ inch pieces.
2. Put meat in pan and just cover with water. Bring to boil and cook for about 5 minutes. Drain.
3. Mix conch and clam chowder together and heat thoroughly. If too thick, add enough water to thin to desired consistency.

WATER CRESS SOUP (2 quarts)

(Mrs. Charles Creighton)

1 cup butter
1 cup chopped celery (with a few leaves)
1 teaspoon salt
1½ cups chopped water cress

1 large white onion, chopped
1 cup flour
9 cups beef stock
½ teaspoon pepper

1. Melt butter in a large saucepan. Saute onion and celery until very tender. Stir in flour and continue cooking over low heat 8 - 10 minutes, stirring constantly.

2. Blend in beef stock, salt and pepper. Simmer 30 minutes.

3. Strain. Stir in water cress.

~~~~~~~~~~~~~~~~

VICHYSSOISE (1½ quarts)

(Mrs. Arch Campbell)

4 medium potatoes
5 chicken bouillon cubes
5 leeks, minced fine
1 cup milk
¼ teaspoon pepper

3 cups boiling water
3 tablespoons butter
1 cup heavy cream
1 teaspoon salt
1 teaspoon paprika

1. Peel and cube potatoes. Place in large saucepan. Add water, bouillon cubes, butter, leeks. Cover pan and cook about 30 minutes (or until potatoes are tender).

2. Press mixture through sieve or blend in blender. Put into saucepan. Add cream, milk, salt, pepper. Mix well.

3. Put in refrigerator and chill. Serve with paprika sprinkled on top and a "dollop" of whipped cream or sour cream.

4. This may also be served very hot.

NOTE: Chicken broth may be used for a richer soup.

GRANDMOTHER'S ALL DAY STEW (about 3½ quarts)

(Mrs. Albert E. Jenner, Jr.)

2½ pounds lean beef, cut fine
1½ cups chopped celery
1 tablespoon salt
1 bay leaf
½ bunch parsley
2 or 3 small marrow bones

2 medium onions
2 tablespoons monosodium
glutemate
Dash of thyme, basil, rosemary,
Marjoram and white pepper

1. In blender mix celery tops and parsley, add onions and spices.

2. Put into large pot, meat, bone, spice mix. Cover with water. Simmer for 3 - 4 hours in covered pot. If it boils down, add a little more water.

3. If potatoes are wanted, dice and add during last half hour of cooking.

NOTE: In a pressure cooker, cook for 1 hour. Freezes well.

CLAM MADRILENE SOUP (serves 6)

(Mrs. Thais Eberts)

3 cups jellied madrilene
Juice of ½ lemon
1 tablespoon chopped chives
⅛ teaspoon dried tarragon
1½ cups clam juice

1 tablespoon chopped fresh
dill
1 teaspoon lemon rind
½ cup sour cream

1. Mix jellied madrilene, clam juice, lemon juice, rind, chives, tarragon, fresh dill. Chill.

2. When ready to serve fold in sour cream.

BRUNSWICK STEW (about 12 quarts)

(Mrs. Clifford H. Allan)

4 pounds fresh pork
4 one pound cans creamed corn
4 one pound cans lima beans
1 pound onions, chopped
½ bottle Worcestershire
4 pounds chicken

4 one pound cans cut okra
4 large cans tomatoes
5 pounds cooked potatoes
2 hot peppers, crushed (or red peppers)

1. Cook meat and chicken in large pot with water to cover until meat falls from bone. Remove from pot. Cut meat into bite-sized pieces, discard bones. Return meat and chicken to pot.
2. Add corn, okra, lima beans, tomatoes, onion, Worcestershire and peppers. Simmer for 10 - 15 minutes (or if using fresh vegetables, simmer until vegetables are tender).
3. Mash cooked potatoes and add to stew. Mix thoroughly.

NOTE: May be frozen. Recipe may be reduced but it is hard to get all ingredients in. If using fresh vegetables instead of canned, stir occasionally from bottom of pot to prevent sticking and burning.

CRAWFISH BISQUE (serves 4)

(Mrs. Tom G. Lively)

2 cooked crawfish tails
4 tablespoons flour
1 teaspoon onion juice
½ cup white wine
⅛ teaspoon pepper

2 cups cream
5 tablespoons butter
1 teaspoon Worcestershire
½ teaspoon salt
Optional: ½ cup mushrooms

1. Melt butter. Add flour, cream, onion juice, Worcestershire and salt. Cook for 5 minutes or until mixture thickens.
2. Cut crawfish into bite-size pieces. Add cooked mushrooms and crawfish to cream mixture. Heat. Stir in wine.
3. Serve in heated cups. Sprinkle pepper on top.

SARAH'S SPLIT PEA SOUP

(Mrs. Arch Campbell)

1 ham bone with approx. 1 cup
  ham meat (left-over bone
  perfect)
½ cup celery, chopped
  with leaves
½ cup carrots, chopped
1 teaspoon leaf thyme

2 quarts water
2 garlic cloves, minced
½ cup onion, chopped
1 tablespoon rendered ham fat
½ teaspoon ground sage
1 pound quick-cook green split
  peas

1. Wash peas in cold water and drain.
2. Melt ham fat in frying pan and saute onions, celery, carrots, garlic, sage, thyme until onions are soft but not brown.
3. In large kettle put water, ham bone (with meat on), peas. Bring to boil. Turn to simmer.
4. Add sauted vegetables and simmer for at least 2 hours stirring occasionally to prevent peas from sticking.
5. Remove ham bone (with meat) and allow bone to cool. Pick meat from bone and cut into less than bite-sized pieces.
6. Puree coarsely the vegetables and peas (may use colander).
7. Return meat and vegetables to soup. If too thick, add enough water to thin to "thick" soup consistency. Re-heat.

FRENCH ONION SOUP (serves 4 - 6)

(Recipe Selection Committee)

1 pound onions
Butter
Dash salt
Dash pepper

3 cups beef stock
1 cup dry white wine
Small pieces of crisp toast
Grated Parmesan cheese

1. Peel onions and slice very thin. Melt butter to cover bottom of pan. Brown onions in butter.
2. Add stock and wine. Simmer about 30 more minutes.
3. Put in large soup tureen or serve in individual soup bowls. Float crisp toast on top of soup and sprinkle with cheese. Serve at once.

FRUIT SOUP

(Kenneth W. Ricklefs)

¼ pound dried prunes
¼ pound dried apples
1 quart water
½ cup sugar
½ cup tapioca

¼ pound dried apricots
Juice of half lemon
Rind of half lemon
1 cinnamon stick

1. Soak fruit in kettle in cold water about 3 hours. Add sugar and cinnamon. Put kettle on fire and cook fruit until tender. Remove fruit to serving dish.

2. Mix tapioca into fruit juice. Cook until done. Add rind and lemon juice. Pour over fruit.

3. Chill in refrigerator. Serve with rusks (biscuits).

NOTE: May be served hot if desired. Instead of tapioca, juice may be thickened with 1 tablespoon cornstarch or 1 tablespoon of potato flour.

FISH CHOWDER (serves 4)

(Recipe Selection Committee

2 pounds fish fillets
2 small onions
Water
1 teaspoon salt

4 medium sized potatoes
2 slices bacon or small piece of salt pork
¼ teaspoon pepper

1. Cut all ingredients into small pieces and put into large pot. Bring to boil. Reduce heat and simmer for about 40 - 50 minutes or until potatoes are falling apart. Stir with spoon, mashing as you stir. Chowder should be thick.

2. Serve hot.

VARIATIONS: Add milk or cream, about 1 cup for the pot. Add 1 can tomato paste or 1 can tomatoes.

INLAND WATERWAY, FORT LAUDERDALE, FLORIDA

Vegetables

Cauliflower is nothing but cabbage with a college education.

Pudd'nhead Wilson's Calendar
Mark Twain
(1835-1910)

EGGPLANT SUPREME (serves 6)

(Mrs. Mary Tsolas)

1 large eggplant (to make about 4 cups eggplant)
1 medium onion, chopped
½ cup milk
½ cup grated Romano cheese

2 tablespoons butter
1 can cream of mushroom soup
2 egg yolks, beaten
¾ cup toasted bread crumbs (or packaged herb stuffing)

1. Peel and dice eggplant. Put in boiling salt water and cook about 5 minutes, or until tender. Drain.
2. Melt butter in saucepan. Add onion and saute slightly.
3. Add soup, milk, egg and cheese. Heat.
4. Add eggplant and crumbs. Toss together to mix.
5. Put into greased baking dish. Sprinkle top with crumbs, dot with butter, sprinkle with salt and pepper.
6. Bake 20 minutes at 350° or until hot and top browned.

EGGPLANT PARMIGIANA (serves 4 - 6)

(Mrs. P. Silvano)

1 large eggplant
2 tablespoons grated Parmesan cheese
½ pound mozzarella cheese sliced thin

2 eggs
2 tablespoons water
Bread crumbs
½ cup salad oil
1½ cups tomato sauce .

1. Wash eggplant. Slice in ¼ inch slices. Sprinkle with salt. Set aside for 1 hour, then drain.
2. Beat eggs with water. Dip eggplant into egg mixture then into dry crumbs.
3. Fry eggplant in oil until brown.
4. Place eggplant in casserole. Cover with tomato sauce. Sprinkle with Parmesan cheese. Add layer of mozzarella cheese.
5. Bake in oven at 400° for about 15 minutes. Serve hot.

FRIED EGG PLANT

(Mrs. Lucian Craig, 1924
Woman's Club Cook Book)

1 firm medium sized egg plant

Batter:
1 tablespoon flour   1 egg
¾ cup evaporated milk

1. Make batter by mixing milk, egg and flour.
2. Wash egg plant, slice into ¼ inch thick slices (do not peel).
3. Immediately dip egg plant slices into batter and fry in hot fat until brown (about 4 minutes each side).
4. Serve at once.

SAUTEED ZUCCHINI

(Mrs. J. A. Haberkorn)

3-4 young zucchini   Paprika
Olive oil   Sweet basil
Dash salt   Optional: dash onion, chopped

1. Scrub zucchini. Slice crosswise into thin slices. Saute in oil which has dash of salt, paprika, sweet basil, onion. Turn often and cook until tender.
2. Serve with tomato sauce.

Tomato Sauce:
1 slice onion   2 stalks celery, chopped with
Parsley   with leaves
½ green pepper, chopped   1 carrot, chopped
2 tablespoons flour   3 tablespoons butter
⅛ teaspoon pepper   ¼ teaspoon salt
2 cups stewed tomatoes   1 teaspoon sugar

1. Cook tomatoes with onion, celery, parsley, carrot and pepper for 15 minutes; strain to make stock.
2. Melt butter in saucepan. Add flour, slowly add stock. Bring to boil. When thick, add salt, pepper, sugar.

GREEN BEANS SUPREME (serves 12)

(Mrs. Grover M. Davis)

3 packages frozen green beans
1 can mushroom soup
¼ teaspoon pepper
1 can sliced mushrooms with ½ juice

1 whole peeled onion
¼ pint sour cream
½ teaspoon Accent
¼ cup slivered almonds
½ cup grated sharp cheese

1. Cook beans with whole onion about 10 minutes in salted water. Drain and remove onion.
2. Put beans in 2 quart casserole. Add soup, cream, pepper, Accent, mushrooms and cheese. Stir. Over top sprinkle the slivered almonds.
3. Bake for 30 minutes at 350°.

GREEN BEANS BROWARD

(Mrs. Thomas J. Newbill)

1 pound fresh green beans
4 tablespoons salted pecan pieces

2 tablespoons toasted onion bits
1 tablespoon bacon fat
2 tablespoons butter

1. Wash, cut beans. Put into salted water to cover. Add bacon fat. Cook 15 - 20 minutes or until tender. Drain.
2. Add pecan pieces, onion bits and butter. Toss and serve.

OKRA AND HOLLANDAISE (serves 4)

(Recipe Selection Committee)

1 cup hot hollandaise sauce   1 pound okra (approx.)

1. Bring salted water to rolling boil.
2. Select only young tender okra. Wash. Do not cut off stem.
3. Drop into boiling water. Return to boil. Boil for 10 minutes. Remove from water at once.
4. Serve with ¼ cup hollandaise sauce per person.

NOTE: The okra is picked up by the stem end and "dunked" into the sauce.

STEAMED OKRA WITH ONIONS AND TOMATOES

(Recipe Selection Committee)

2 medium onions, chopped fine
1 pound okra
¼ cup water

4 tomatoes, sliced
1 tablespoon butter
Dash salt
Dash pepper

1. Wash okra. Remove stems and slice.
2. Put butter, water, onion in saucepan. Cover and cook about 15 minutes or until onions are tender. Watch and if water boils away, add a little more.
3. Put okra on top of the cooked onions, then layer of tomatoes. Sprinkle with salt and pepper.
4. Put cover on tightly and simmer slowly for 15-20 minutes.

GRETCHEN'S CARROTS

(Mrs. Magnus Loftstedt)

¼ cup butter
2 tablespoons parsley, chopped
1 tablespoon flour

6 or 7 medium sized carrots
¼ teaspoon salt

1. Slice carrots as you would French string beans.
2. Melt butter in frying pan. Toss carrots in butter for about 5 minutes, or until coated with butter.
3. Add flour and mix in thoroughly. Add parsley.
4. Add enough boiling water to cover and simmer about 20 minutes. Add salt.

FRIED AKEE

(Recipe Selection Committee)

1. Use fleshy part of fruit. Boil in salted water for 5 minutes. Remove from water and dry. Discard water.
2. In fry pan melt butter. Drop akee into pan and fry until brown.

NOTE: A favorite dish of the islands is fried akee and fish.

SPINACH CASSEROLE

(Mrs. Mildred Moore)

2 10 ounce packages of frozen spinach (or 2 pounds fresh)
½ pound sliced bacon
1 teaspoon salt
1½ cups shredded Cheddar cheese

2 cups milk
2 eggs
⅔ cup soft bread crumbs

1. Dice bacon and fry until crisp. Drain on paper towel.
2. Cook spinach and drain thoroughly.
3. Slightly beat eggs, add milk, salt, bread crumbs, half of the cheese, and the bacon.
4. Pour into 1½ quart baking dish. Sprinkle remaining cheese in 2 inch border around top of spinach. Sprinkle paprika in center if desired.
5. Bake 30 minutes at 375° or until mixture is thoroughly heated.

~~~~~~~~~~~~~~

CUCUMBER ICE

(Recipe Selection Committee)

2 large cucumbers
1½ cups boiling water

½ cup sugar
2 egg whites

1. Grate cucumbers which have been peeled or not, as you wish into large bowl. Put sugar into boiling water until dissolved. Pour over cucumbers.
2. Beat egg whites until stiff. Fold in cucumber mix.
3. Put in deep freeze until edges set. Remove and mix well. Pour back into tray or bowl and put in freezer. Do not freeze "hard as a rock".

NOTE: Wonderful with fish dishes.

PIGEON PEAS AND RICE, NASSAU STYLE

(Mrs. Ann M. Perry)

1 cup dried pigeon peas
(soaked overnight and
drained) or 2 cups freshly
shelled green peas
1 pound lean pork, diced
½ cup salad oil
1 chopped onion

1 cup tomato sauce
1 bunch parsley, chopped
Bay leaves
2 teaspoons salt
½ teaspoon black pepper
¼ cup rice, washed and drained

1. In saucepan cover peas with fresh water, add diced pork, salt, pepper and chopped parsley. Cook over low heat until tender (about 2 hours for dried peas). Add hot water as often as necessary to prevent burning.

2. Put salad oil in fry pan, heat, add onions and saute for about 10 minutes, stirring often. Add tomato sauce, bay leaves. Simmer 5 minutes more.

3. Pour mixture over pigeon peas. Add 1½ cups water and bring to rolling boil.

4. Stir in rice and cook 25 minutes more or until rice is done. Add small amount of hot water to prevent burning if necessary.

CABBAGE WITH HAM

(Recipe Selection Committee)

1 head cabbage
2 cups cut up cooked ham

2 cups tiny white onions
Water
Salt

1. In large pot put onions and ham. Cover with salted water. Cook until onions are tender (or about 20 minutes).

2. Cut cabbage head into 8 wedges. Lay cabbage in pot of ham and onions. Be sure there is enough water to prevent burning. Bring to boil. Put lid on pot. Boil for 10 minutes.

ORANGE PEAS

(Mrs. Arch Campbell)

1 package peas
2 tablespoons butter
1 teaspoon cornstarch

1 orange (enough to make ½ cup orange juice and ½ teaspoon of orange rind)

1. Cook peas as instructed on package, but use ½ cup orange juice instead of water. Add butter, rind and cornstarch.
2. Cook for 7 minutes or until sauce on peas is thick.

CHAYOTES AU GRATIN

(Recipe Selection Committee)

2 chayotes
Butter

1 cup thick white sauce
½ cup grated cheese

1. Peel chayote, then slice. Put into water to cover. Add dash salt. Cook about 20 minutes or until tender but not mushy.
2. Put chayote in buttered baking dish. Pour white sauce over, top with cheese and dots of butter.
3. Bake at 350° for about 15 minutes or until cheese is brown.

FRIED CHAYOTE

(Recipe Selection Committee)

1. Select ripe chayote. Peel, remove seed and dice flesh.
2. Melt butter in fry pan. Put chayote into pan and cook until tender, turning often. Do not have pan too hot.

GRITS (serves 4)

(Recipe Selection Committee)

1 cup washed grits   1 teaspoon salt
4 cups water

1. Bring salted water to a boil. Add grits slowly so that boiling does not stop. Stir.
2. Cover and let cook about 40 minutes. Stir often.
3. Serve hot with butter.

GRITS FRITTERS

(Mrs. B. A. Cromartie)

2 cups cooked grits (cold)   1 egg
1 heaping tablespoon flour   1 teaspoon baking powder
Dash salt   Cooking oil
Dash pepper

1. Mash grits and mix with egg, flour, salt, pepper and baking powder.
2. Heat deep oil in fry pan. Drop grits mixture from spoon into hot fat. Fry to golden brown stage. Drain on paper towel.

BOILED HEART OF PALM (Swamp Cabbage)

(Recipe Selection Committee)

4 cups sliced or chopped   Bacon
  Heart of Palm   1 teaspoon salt
½ teaspoon pepper   Hollandaise sauce

1. Place sliced Heart of Palm in pan. Cover with salted water. Add pepper. Bring to boil. Reduce heat and simmer until tender. (About 30 - 40 minutes with lid on pan.) Check occasionally. If water evaporates, add only enough to prevent sticking.
2. Serve at once with lump of butter, or with hollandaise sauce. For variety, cook with bacon.

SOUTHERN SWEET POTATOES

(Mrs. G. Sayre Fitzpatrick)

6 medium sized potatoes
1 stick butter
4 tablespoons bourbon

1½ cups brown sugar
½ cup water

1. Cook potatoes in boiling water until slightly tender (about 45 minutes).
2. Peel potatoes and cut in half.
3. Place potatoes in shallow baking dish and add the butter, water and brown sugar.
4. Bake at 450° for about 30 minutes (or until bubbly and candied).
5. Remove from oven. Pour bourbon over potatoes. Cover and let stand for a minute. Serve at once.

SWEET POTATO PONE

(Mrs. Hal M. Caudle, Sr.)

1 quart raw grated new sweet potatoes
¾ cup cane syrup
1 cup milk
½ teaspoon nutmeg

¾ teaspoon salt
1 egg
3 tablespoons melted butter
½ cup flour
1 teaspoon cinnamon

1. Sift together flour, salt, cinnamon, nutmeg.
2. Mix egg, cane syrup, butter, milk and potato. Mix into flour mixture.
3. Pour into buttered baking dish and bake at 275° for about 2 hours, stirring occasionally. Bake for 30 minutes longer without stirring and allowing pone to brown.
4. May be served hot or cold.

NOTE: Variation: Add 1 cup of persimmon pulp when adding eggs. Makes a softer pone and a delightfully different flavor. Serve with pork or other meat.

HARVARD BEETS (serves 4)

(Mrs. Kenneth Richardson, 1924
Woman's Club Cook Book)

12 small beets
½ tablespoon cornstarch
2 tablespoons butter

½ cup sugar
½ cup vinegar

1. Wash beets. Cook in boiling water until soft. (About 20 minutes).
2. Remove skin from beets. Cut into small cubes.
3. Mix cornstarch and sugar. Add vinegar. Bring mixture to a boil.
4. Pour mixture over beets and let stand for at least ½ hour.
5. Heat and serve.

BEETS WITH ORANGE SAUCE

(Recipe Selection Committee)

1 tablespoon butter
1½ tablespoons cornstarch
Rind of ½ orange
2½ cups diced cooked beets

4 tablespoons brown sugar
¾ cup orange juice
Dash salt
Dash pepper

1. In saucepan melt butter, add sugar and cornstarch. Stirring constantly add orange juice and rind. Cook until thick. Add salt, pepper and beets.
2. Serve at once or can be cooled and re-heated. (Be careful not to burn it while re-heating.)

COLLARD GREENS

(Recipe Selection Committee)

1. Select young and tender collard greens. Wash and cut fine.
2. Cover with salted water. Cook one hour.
3. Serve at table with broth in which greens have been cooked. This is the "pot liquor".
4. If desired, a strip of bacon may be added after 30 minutes of cooking.

NOTE: Serve with cornbread to "dunk" in the "pot liquor".

WILD RICE WITH CELERY

(Welcom H. Watson)

1½ cups wild rice
Dash salt
Dash pepper

1 cup celery crescents
2 tablespoons butter

1. Cook rice according to directions on package.
2. Cut celery crosswise to make crescents.
3. Soak celery in boiling salted water for 15 minutes or until just tender. Drain.
4. If any water left on rice, drain.
5. Toss rice, celery, salt, pepper and butter.

~~~~~~~~~~~~~~~~~~~~~~~~~

HEAVENLY RICE (serves 4 - 6)

(Mrs. Charles Schwarm)

1 stick butter
1 cup chopped onion

1 cup long grain rice
2 cans undiluted bouillon

1. Melt butter in skillet and brown rice and onion.
2. In saucepan boil undiluted bouillon
3. Put rice and onion in casserole dish and pour hot bouillon over them.
4. Cook for one hour at 350°.

~~~~~~~~~~~~~~~~~~~~~~~~~

OVEN COOKED RICE

(Mrs. Nelson B. Thomas)

1 cup uncooked rice
1 teaspoon salt

1 cup water
1 tablespoon butter

1. Wash and drain rice.
2. Place rice, water, salt and butter in baking dish. Stir.
3. Cover and bake at 350° for 30 minutes.

WILD RICE CASSEROLE

(Mrs. George H. Kittredge, Jr.)

2 cups uncooked wild rice
2 cans beef consomme with 2
cans water
1 can mushrooms

1½ sticks butter
1 medium bell pepper, minced
1 medium onion, minced
Salt to taste

1. Saute onions, pepper, rice in butter until browned.
2. Add consomme, water, mushrooms. Mix.
3. Pour into casserole and bake for 45 minutes at 375°.
   Stir occasionally with fork while baking.

PILAF (serves 6)

(Mrs. Nelson B. Thomas)

2 cans undiluted beef bouillon
1 medium onion, chopped
2 3½ ounce cans mushroom
pieces

1 cup uncooked long cooking
rice
⅔ stick butter

1. Brown mushrooms and onion in skillet.
2. Mix rice and bouillon in large ungreased casserole.
3. Add mushroom-onion mix to the. rice.
4. Cover dish and bake at 300° for 1½ hours. Stir every
   half hour.

RICE CAKES

(Recipe Selection Committee)

1 cup cooked rice
1 teaspoon baking powder
2 eggs

1 cup flour
1 cup milk
½ teaspoon salt

1. Separate eggs. Mix yolks with milk. Mix flour, salt, baking
   powder and rice, then mix yolk mixture with rice mixture.
2. Beat egg whites until stiff. Fold into rice mixture. Form
   into patty shape.
3. Grease fry pan and heat. Drop rice patties on pan and
   brown on both sides.

BROCCOLI SOUFFLE

(Miss Nola G. Bates)

1 cup chopped frozen broccoli
3 tablespoons flour
3 eggs

2 tablespoons butter
1 cup milk
¼ teaspoon onion juice

1. Melt butter in pan, add flour, milk to make white sauce. Cook until thick.

2. Separate eggs. Mix yolks into white sauce and cook for 1 minute more. Do not boil. Add finely chopped broccoli, onion juice and cool mixture.

3. Beat egg whites until stiff. Fold into broccoli mixture.

4. Pour into greased baking pan and set pan in dish of hot water.

5. Bake at 350° until firm, about 25 - 35 minutes.

NOTE: Same recipe may be used for spinach or zucchini.

~~~~~~~~~~~~

CREOLE KRAUT

(Mrs. W. W. Lundy)

1 large can sauerkraut
¼ teaspoon salt
3 tablespoons diced bell pepper
3 tablespoons kraut juice
½ teaspoon Tabasco sauce
(optional)

1 large can tomatoes
6 tablespoons diced raw bacon
3 tablespoons diced onion
1½ tablespoons flour

1. Drain kraut saving out 3 tablespoons of the juice.

2. Combine tomatoes, salt, bacon, pepper and onion. Boil slowly for about 15 minutes.

3. Mix kraut juice and flour. Add to tomato mixture and cook until thickens slightly. Add Tabasco if desired.

4. Add kraut. Simmer for 30 minutes, or place in oven at 350° for 30 minutes.

STUFFED PEPPERS (serves 5)

(Mrs. Burns A. Dobbins, Jr.)

1 pound ground beef
1 cup bread crumbs
½ small onion, chopped fine
Cooking oil

10 green peppers
1 No. 2 can tomatoes
1 package of peanuts, ground
(or 2 tablespoons peanut
butter)

1. Brown meat in oil. Add onion, tomatoes and cook until tomatoes are well cooked. Add bread crumbs and peanuts, and a dash of salt.
2. Wash peppers. Using sharp knife cut out blossom end and seed core.
3. Fill peppers with meat mixture. Place in shallow baking pan. Bake for 1 hour at 350°.

BLACK BEANS

(Recipe Selection Committee)

1 pound black beans
2 medium diced onions
3 tablespoons vinegar
¼ teaspoon salt
¼ teaspoon oregano

1 diced green pepper
1 clove garlic
4 tablespoons olive oil
¼ teaspoon pepper

1. Soak beans overnight in large pot. Next morning put pot on stove and simmer 2 - 3 hours, or until tender.
2. In fry pan put oil. Add pepper, onion and sliced garlic. Fry until tender.
3. Add fried ingredients to beans. Add salt, pepper, vinegar and oregano.
4. Cook slowly about 30 minutes. Use spoon to stir with a mashing action so that some of the beans are crushed. This thickens the mixture.

NOTE: Tastes better after standing. Store in refrigerator.

BAKED BEANS

(Mrs. Earl J. Meiers)

1½ pounds (approx.) Great Northern beans
¼ cup brown sugar
1 tablespoon minced onion

¼ pound salt pork
½ cup molasses
¼ cup catsup

1. Soak beans overnight in water to cover.
2. Keeping same water, cook beans about 1 hour.
3. In saucepan boil salt pork which has been cut into cubes for about ½ hour. Drain and throw away water.
4. In baking pan put beans with the cooking water, salt pork, molasses, brown sugar, onion and catsup. Mix.
5. Bake at 325° for about 2½ hours. Check to make sure beans do not bake dry. Add a little water if necessary.

FRENCH FRIED ONION RINGS

(Mrs. Arch Campbell)

4 to 5 large mild onions
3 eggs

2 cups milk
1 cup flour (approx.)

1. Slice large onions very thin.
2. In flat pan beat eggs and add milk. Mix well.
3. In second flat pan spread flour.
4. Put only one handful of onion rings into milk mix. Swish around to make sure each ring is wet. Lift rings and shake lightly to remove some of the moisture.
5. Drop rings into flour. Swish around making sure each ring is covered with flour.
6. Drop floured rings into hot deep fat (450°). Lightly stir to separate pieces and to insure each one browning. A fryer basket is helpful. Left out rings and place on paper toweling to drain.
7. Start over again with step 4. It is important to do only a few rings at a time.

SUPER ONIONS (serves 6)

(Mrs. Dwight L. Rogers, Sr.)

2 1 pound cans onions
½ cup coarsely grated Cheddar
  cheese

1 can condensed cream of
  celery soup
¼ cup chopped almonds

1. Drain onions well and put in one quart casserole.
2. Gently stir in soup. Sprinkle top with cheese and almonds.
3. Bake 20 to 25 minutes at 375°.

～～～～～～～～～～～

MORINGA LEAF AND BLOSSOM CURRY

(Mrs. Ann M. Perry)

Moringa leaves and blossoms
Chopped crisp bacon or ham

Butter
Dash salt
Dash pepper

1. Gather moringa leaves and flowers early in morning. Wash and remove tough stems.
2. In steamer, steam until tender with little or no additional water.
3. To serve add salt, pepper, butter and chopped crisp bacon or ham. Toss and serve at once.

～～～～～～～～～～～

ARTICHOKES (serves 4)

(Recipe Selection Committee)

4 artichokes
1 clove garlic, slivered

2 cups wine
4 teaspoons olive oil

1. Trim 1 inch from top of each artichoke. Remove stem and bottom leaves. Tuck a sliver of garlic into each heart.
2. Stand upright in heavy pan. Put 1 teaspoon olive oil on each artichoke. Add wine. Cover with tight lid.
3. Simmer for about 45 minutes or until tender. Drain.
4. Serve immediately with hot hollandaise sauce or, chill and serve with cold hollandaise sauce.

NOTE: Salted boiling water may be substituted for the wine.

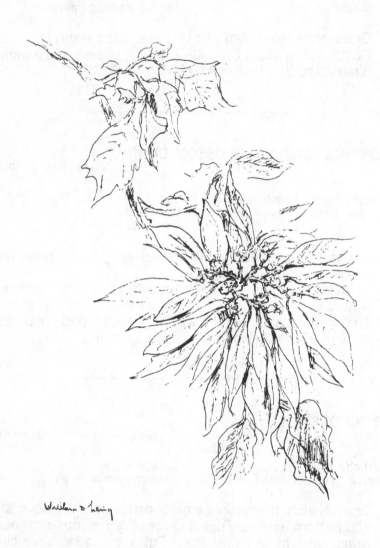

POINSETTIAS, FORT LAUDERDALE, FLORIDA

Cookery Hints
and Tricks

Cookery is become an art, a noble science; . . . .

Anatomy of Melancholy. The Author's Abstract

Robert Burton

(1577-1640)

COOKERY HINTS AND TRICKS

BAKING POWDER —

To make homemade baking powder, use one pound of cream of tartar and mix with one pound of flour. Push through sieve 3 or 4 times. Store in dry place. Use 1 teaspoon of homemade baking powder to 1 cup of flour when baking.

COCONUT —

Ways to open:

1. Drive husk down onto spike and twist. Follow a straight line around husk. You should be able to twist brown nut out of husk.

2. Use hand hatchet and chop off husk. Peel out nut.

3. Use electric saw and saw off husk.

4. Use monkey method - climb very high tree. When you get to top, drop coconut onto rock. Climb down and find the pieces.

To get meat out of brown shell:

1. Use nail to punch "eyes." Drain over glass. Use hammer and give shell several hard knocks. Use chisel or screw driver, crack shell. Use short-bladed sturdy knife to lift out meat.

2. Punch "eyes" to drain. Use electric saw and make several cuts in shell. Pry open. Use short-bladed sturdy knife to lift out meat.

Use moist coconut in pies. Grate fresh coconut and add to your creamed pies. If using for topping on cakes place in open dish in refrigerator to dry out. (Mrs. Albert Frederick)

COFFEE —

To roast your coffee, use heavy bottomed skillet. Mix about 1 teaspoon of butter with 1 teaspoon of sugar. Melt in bottom of pan. Add about 1 pound of green coffee beans. Brown beans by shaking and stirring constantly. If beans should "pop" or smoke, shake faster. When all brown, remove, cool and store. They may be ground for immediate use. Note: Butter and sugar are said to help improve the flavor and aroma of the coffee. Care should be taken not to use too much butter and sugar.

COOKIES —

To keep cookies fresh and crisp in a container, cut a piece of apple and store it with baked cookies.

FISH —

To draw out the salt from salted fish, add a glass of vinegar to the water in which the salt fish is soaking.

FRUIT —

To peel an orange easily, and to get the skin off in one piece, heat the orange slightly for three or four minutes before peeling. Heat lemons well before using and there will be twice the quantity of juice.

Rolling a lemon on table like a rolling pin will give you more juice.

JAM —

When making jam, rub the bottom of pan with butter. This prevents burning and keeps the jam clear.

NUTS —

To remove the kernels whole from pecan nuts, pour boiling water over the nuts and let them stand until cold. Then hammer on the small end of the nut.

Store nuts in plastic container in freezer to keep fresh.

PIES —

Put a bit of lime juice in **every fruit** pie. (From Mrs. George F. Young who got this hint from her grandmother, Mrs. Dewitt Ten-Brook)

PINEAPPLE —

The easiest way to peel pineapple is to lay it down on chop board. Grab by green leaves (use gloves if too pricky). Use very sharp knife, slice off pieces as you would slice bread. Then, chop off brown skin from each slice. Use paring knife, cut out eyes.

POPCORN ROPES —

Make one dishpan full of popcorn. Use needle threaded with heavy cotton thread. While popcorn is still warm, push needle through thickest part. Tie loop at beginning and end of rope of popcorn. Each rope should be about 5 feet long. After Christmas, hang ropes in yard for birds to eat.

POMANDER BALL —

Using a needle, run a piece of fine wire through an orange. Make a small loop. This is just a "hanging device." Using whole cloves, push cloves into orange until orange is covered with the cloves. Run pretty ribbon through loop. Tie some little bows on the orange here and there. Hang in closet or where ever you wish. As the orange dries out, it has a nice spicy odor.

SOUP —

When making soup remember the maxim: Soup boiled is soup spoiled. Soup should be cooked gently and evenly.

Grate a raw potato and add it to your soup when too much salt has been added.

SPAGHETTI —

For cooking spaghetti, macaroni, noodles: Bring large kettle to boiling point, add salt (as called for on package). Bring to rolling boil.

Put in boiling water, stir and put tight lid on kettle. Turn off heat and let stand for 20 minutes. They will be cooked perfectly.

Drain. Plunge into **cold** water and store in refrigerator in covered container in water for use up to three days later. (Mrs. W. Lemkau)

1 teaspoon butter added to boiling water will prevent noodles, spaghetti or macaroni from boiling over side.

VEGETABLES —

For those who love onions but have trouble eating them - soak onions in milk (just to cover) for about 1 hour, covered, in refrigerator.

To peel onion place under cold water while peeling and no tears.

To bake potatoes quickly, boil them in salted water for ten minutes, then put them into the oven and bake. Boiling water will heat them through more readily.

Lemon juice or vinegar in the water cauliflower is cooked in makes it keep its snowy white color.

If cereal or vegetables burn, plunge the vessel containing the burned mass into cold water and allow it to remain for a few minutes before pouring the contents into another pan. The burned taste will nearly disappear.

To keep a head of lettuce crisp and fresh, slice head in half and immerse it in ice cold water and cover entire head. This can remain in refrigerator for a week. Just remove the crisp leaves as you need them.

WHIPPED CREAM —

When cream will not whip, add the white of an egg to your cream, chill and it will whip.

SAFE SUBSTITUTES

Butter	Equal amount of margarine
1 cup fresh sweet milk	½ cup evaporated milk plus ½ cup water
1 cup fresh sweet milk	¼ cup dried milk powder plus 1 cup of water plus 2 tablespoons of fat or oil
1 cup fresh sweet milk	1 cup skim milk plus 2 tablespoons fat or oil
1 cup sour milk	1 cup fresh sweet milk plus 1⅓ tablespoons of vinegar (you may substitute lemon or lime juice for the vinegar)
1 ounce (1 square) unsweetened baking chocolate	3 tablespoons cocoa plus one tablespoon butter
1 tablespoon of flour for thickening	½ tablespoon cornstarch
1 cup honey	¾ cup sugar plus ¼ cup water
½ cup molassas	½ cup dark corn syrup
1 - 10 ounce package frozen sliced strawberries	1 cup fresh sliced strawberries with ⅓ cup of sugar
1 - 12 ounce package frozen peaches	1⅓ cup fresh sliced peaches with ⅓ cup sugar
½ cup seedless raisins	½ cup cut-up dried prunes
½ pound fresh mushrooms	1 can (4 oz) mushrooms

INLAND WATERWAY, FORT LAUDERDALE, FLORIDA

WEIGHTS, MEASURES AND EQUIVALENTS

Dash .... Less than ⅛ teaspoon

3 teaspoons .... 1 tablespoon

4 tablespoons .... ¼ cup

16 tablespoons .... 1 cup

1 cup .... ½ pint

2 cups .... 1 pint

2 cups liquid .... 1 pound

Butter: 2 tablespoons .... 1 ounce
      ½ stick .... ¼ cup
      1 stick .... ½ cup
      2 sticks .... 1 cup
      1 pound .... 2 cups

Chocolate: 1 ounce Baker's .... 1 square

Coffee: 3 ounces coffee .... 1 cup

Egg: 8 large eggs .... 1 pound
     9 medium eggs .... 1 pound
     12-13 egg whites .... 1½ cups whites

Flour: 4½ ounces flour .... 1 unsifted cup
     3¾ ounces .... 1 sifted cup
     4 cups .... 1 pound

Lemon: Juice of 1 medium .... 3 tablespoons

Meat: 2 cups, chopped .... 1 pound

Milk: 8 ounces .... 1 cup

Molasses: 11 ounces .... 1 cup

Rice: 7 ounces .... 1 cup

Sugar, Brown: 2⅔ cups .... 1 pound
     Powdered: 2⅔ cups .... 1 pound
     White: 8 ounces .... 1 cup
     White: 2 cups .... 1 pound

Tea: 2 ounces .... 1 cup

INDEX

239

AFTERWORD TO THE FOURTH EDITION

In 1984, as the Fort Lauderdale Historical Society's Fundraising Committee began the planning for a new edition of *Fort Lauderdale Recipes*, major revisions and updating were considered. Since the cookbook was first published, more food products are available, as are many new food preparation techniques. Restaurant cuisine, in particular, has become very sophisticated and has brought Fort Lauderdale a national reputation for fine food.

Despite these factors, it was the consensus of those consulted that the original edition remained an outstanding regional cookbook and should be reprinted unchanged. Many of the recipes for locally grown products are unavailable elsewhere. We hope you will enjoy them.

Fundraising Committee
Fort Lauderdale Historical Society

NOTES

NOTES

NOTES

NOTES

NOTES

NOTES

NOTES

NOTES

NOTES

NOTES

NOTES

NOTES

NOTES

NOTES

NOTES